TEXAS IRON
GUNS OF THE TEXAS RANGERS

ROBERT D. MOSER

Copyright © 2017
By Robert D. Moser
Published By Wild Horse Press
An Imprint of Wild Horse Media Group
P.O. Box 331779
Fort Worth, Texas 76163
1-817-344-7036
www.WildHorseMedia.com
ALL RIGHTS RESERVED
1 2 3 4 5 6 7 8 9
ISBN-10: 1-68179-105-6
ISBN-13: 978-1-68179-105-0

ALL RIGHTS RESERVED. No part of this book may be reproduced in any form without written permission from the publisher, except for brief passages included in a review appearing in a newspaper or magazine.

To Adine, my wife,
who has been
my inspiration.

TABLE OF CONTENTS

Preface		7
Introduction		9
List of illustrations		13
CHAPTER 1	Arms of the Colony	17
CHAPTER 2	Arming the Republic	25
CHAPTER 3	War with Mexico	33
CHAPTER 4	The Time Between the Wars	41
CHAPTER 5	The Civil War	51
CHAPTER 6	The Time of Reconstruction	61
CHAPTER 7	Time of the Outlaw	69
CHAPTER 8	Racing toward the Century	79
CHAPTER 9	Rangers and the Cavalry	89
CHAPTER 10	Turning of the Century	97
CHAPTER 11	Time of the Gangster	107
CHAPTER 12	Post WW II Years	117
CHAPTER 13	Bar-B-Q Guns	127
CHAPTER 14	Commemoratives and Special Edition Firearms	137
CHAPTER 15	Favorites	145
CHAPTER 16	Stories I Forgot to Tell	153
CHAPTER 17	Modern Era Ranger Guns	165
CHAPTER 18	Badges and Handcuffs	179

PREFACE

I have always admired the Texas Rangers and have read many books on their history and sacrifices made in the settlement of our great state. It has been said that more books have been written about the Texas Rangers than any other law enforcement group in history. I have read many of them and what I noticed was that I have yet to come across a book that specifically dedicates its subject matter to the firearms carried and utilized. While reading historical accounts of Rangers conflicts with savage Indians and Mexican bandits, I wondered what weapons were used. Modern TV and motion pictures are starting to use period correct firearms in their productions. This was not always the case. I remember watching westerns depicting the 1860s to 1870s time period carrying Winchester Model 1894 carbines which had not yet been produced. Now it is common to see the Winchester Model 1866 yellow boy being used. The point being that a Rangers ability to accomplish his tasks depended on the type weapon and its reliability. No Ranger regardless of how brave or accomplished could have tamed the Texas frontier without a reliable handgun and rifle. Although not a comprehensive study, this book is written to help bring light to this seldom mentioned area of historical significance. We see many pictures of Rangers wearing pistols and holding carbines but what exactly were they carrying and how did they fit into the puzzle that was taming the Nueces Strip and other turbulent areas. From the time of the Texas Republic up to and including modern times, small arms played a major role in protecting our great state. It is the purpose of this book to highlight this often forgotten subject matter.

INTRODUCTION

One of the greatest privileges I was granted was to pin on the Badge of a Texas Ranger. I have met many good friends over the years as a U.S. Army soldier, Texas Highway patrolman, DPS narcotics investigator and Texas Ranger. If I had not survived my time in Viet Nam, all the good things that followed would not have come about. Bob Moser is a good friend of mine and a fellow front line combat soldier. He flew the Cobra attack helicopter in an Air Cavalry Troop (C trp. 16th Cav.) stationed in Can Tho, RVN. I know that he or members from his Cavalry Troop came to our rescue during life and death situations in the Mekong Delta. At this time, I was serving as a radioman in a unit that we now refer to as a special operations team. Our area of operation was in the Military Region 4, Mekong Delta region of the Republic of South Viet Nam. Serving in this unit I was more than once pinned down by superior enemy fire. When we called for gun support, Bob Moser or pilots from his troop came to our aid and turned the tide of battle. We have become good friends and share the Vietnam experience.

Bob comes from a Texas Ranger heritage. His mother was an Armstrong related to the Honored Ranger Lt. John B. Armstrong of Captain Leander McNelly's Special Frontier Rangers (1875-1879). Bob is a qualified weapons historian and has written numerous articles for the Former Texas Ranger Foundation magazine *Straight Talk*. His articles have received a very positive response from our members. He is highly knowledgeable on the subject of Texas Ranger firearms and has a large number of Rangers documented guns in his personal collection.

I am looking forward to the release of his first book, *Texas Iron, Guns of the Texas Rangers*. This book will be one of the first written on the specific topic of firearms carried by the Texas Rangers. Bob is a very good friend and I wish him the very best on his first book.

– *Johnnie Aycock*
Texas Ranger, Retired

ENDORSEMENTS

H. Joaquin Jackson
The Ranger - Investigations
1010 N. Bird St.
Alpine, Texas 79830
09-26-15

Robert D Moser is a close friend and above all is a friend of all Rangers, his knowledge of Rangers and their weapons is top of the line. His new book, TEXAS IRON. Guns of the Texas Rangers will be accurate and above all a historical piece of work. It will be a must read for anyone who Loves Texas and its Rangers.

Bob Moser is a Texas Hero in his own, having flown attack helicopters the Air Cobra in Vietnam in heavy combat areas, saving many lives of our troops on the ground. God Bless him and the ones like him, and the ones who did not come home.

H. JOAQUIN JACKSON

Retired Texas Ranger
Company "D" Company "E"
1966-1993

Straight Talk, the news magazine of the former Texas Rangers Association, is fortunate to have Bob Moser, Capt. USA, Retired as the FTRA Weapons Historian. His well researched and documented articles add a welcome dimension to the continuing history of the Texas Rangers.

– *Ramiro "Ray" Martinez*
Texas Ranger, Retired

I have enjoyed Bob Moser's articles on "Guns of the Texas Rangers" in our Former Texas Ranger magazine, *Straight Talk*. It is evident that he is highly knowledgeable on historic firearms and their use by the Texas Rangers. I wish him the best of luck with his current book.

– *Carl Weathers*, Captain
Texas Rangers, (Ret)

LIST OF ILLUSTRATIONS

1-1	Plains Rifle	22
1-2	Early flintlock fowling piece	23
1-3	U.S. Model 1816 flintlock pistol	23
1-4	U.S. Model 1836 flintlock pistol	24
1-5	Bowie knife	24
2-1	Paterson Colt	30
2-2	Paterson Colt remake	31
2-3	U.S. Model 1816 musket	31
2-4	Colt Paterson carbine and pistol patent	32
3-1	U.S. Model 1836 flintlock pistol	38
3-2	U.S. Model 1842 percussion pistol	39
3-3	Walker Colt	39
3-4	U.S. First Model Dragoon	40
4-1	Colt Model 1849 pocket / Colt Baby Dragoon	46
4-2	Colt 1851 Navy	47
4-3	Colt Root revolver	48
4-4	Colt Model 1855 carbine	49
4-5	Colt Second Model Dragoon	50
5-1	Colt Model 1860 Army	56
5-2	Remington New Army revolver	57
5-3	Starr Army revolvers	57
5-4	C Sharps rifle/carbine	58
5-5	Grouping of Civil War carbines	59
5-6	Henry Model 1860 rifle	60
6-1	Colt 1860 Army Conversion/1851 Navy Conversion	66
6-2	Smith & Wesson First Model American	66
6-3	Eli Whitney Pocket revolver	67
6-4	Winchester 1866 Yellow boy carbine	67
6-5	Winchester 1873 carbine	68
7-1	Colt Open top 1871	74
7-2	Adams revolver	75
7-3	Merwin Holbert & Co. revolver	75
7-4	Colt Single action Army (Lt Armstrong)	76
7-5	Double barrel Parker Carriage gun	77
7-6	Double barrel Wesley Richards shotgun	78
8-1	Colt DA Model 1877	84

8-2	Winchester 1873 rifle/ Colt SAA in 38/40	84
8-3	Winchester 1892/ Colt SAA in 44/40	85
8-4	Winchester 1876	85
8-5	Colt DA Model 1878	86
8-6	Remington Model 1875 / 1890 revolvers	87
8-7	Winchester Mode 1887 shotgun	88
9-1	Calvary Trooper shell jacket	94
9-2	Colt Model 1873	95
9-3	7 ½ barrel cavalry Colts	96
9-4	U.S. Springfield Model 1873 45/70 "Trapdoor"	96
10-1	Colt Bisley Model SAA	102
10-2	Colt Bisley SAA grouping (barrels 4 ¾, 5 ½ and 7 ½ inches)	103
10-3	Colt Bisley SAA (1906) Texas Ranger Duke Hudson	103
10-4	Colt 1908 hammerless	104
10-5	Winchester Model1886 rifle, 50/110 express	104
10-6	Winchester M1894 Lightweight rifle	105
10-7	Winchester M1894 rifle/carbine	105
10-8	Colt DA 1878 "Alaskan" model	106
10-9	Colt 1911 Commercial 1918	106
11-1	Colt Model 1911's (1920's era)	112
11-2	Colt .380 pocket hammerless	113
11-3	Winchester Model 1907 semi automatic rifle	114
11-4	Remington Model 81 semi automatic rifle	114
11-5	Smith & Wesson 1st Model M&P .38 Special	115
11-6	Colt DA New Army revolver (1906)	115
11-7	Remington Model 10A pump shotgun	116
12-1	Colt Woodsman . 22 National Match Bullseye	122
12-2	Smith & Wesson Model 586 .357 magnum	122
12-3	Remington pump shotgun 870 Wingmaster (DPS)	123
12-4	Winchester Model 1907 Semi loader (Capt Jack Dean)	123
12-5	Smith & Wesson pre model 10 revolver (DPS)	124
12-6	Remington M81 semi-auto rifle, Texas Ranger Byron Currin	124
12-7	2 DPS issued shot guns, Dockery	125
12-8	M-4 Carbine	125
12-9	U.S. Army WW II M1911 A1	126
12-10	Colt Lightweight Commander .45 ACP (two tone)	126
13-1	Colt Lightweight Commander .45 ACP (Clint Peoples)	132
13-2	Colt SAA .45 L/C made 1884 (Jim Nance)	133
13-3	Colt Python .357 magnum (Jim Conrad)	133
13-4	U.S. Army, WW II M1911 A1 (Remington Rand 1943)	134
13-5	Colt M1911 (mfg 1918) fully engraved	134
13-6	Colt SAA, 38/40, 1906, engraved	135
13-7	Colt SAA, 45 l/c, 1900, Cole Agee engraved	135
13-8	Colt SAA, 38/40, 1904 deep cattle brand engraved	136

13-9	Ruger Vaquero, .45 l/c, engraved by former Texas Ranger Peter Maskunas	136
14-1	Charlie Schreiner III Texas Ranger Commemorative	142
14-2	Smith & Wesson 27-2, DPSOA (Weldon Lucas)	142
14-3	Photograph, Weldon Lucas Texas Ranger/Sheriff	142
14-4	Sig Sauer Special Texas Ranger configuration 1911 (Brantley Foster)	143
14-5	FTRF Special Edition Colt Commander	143
14-6	FTRF 45th Commemorative 1911 45ACP 70 series	143
14-7	Texas Ranger 175th Commemorative pair	144
14-8	Texas Ranger SAA, Texas Ranger Calvin J. (Buster) Collins	144
15-1	Taurus PT1911, .45 ACP (Texas Ranger Johnny Aycock, Ret)	148
15-2	Winchester Model 1894 Lever action 30/30 carbine	148
15-3	Photograph–Johnnie Aycock Texas Ranger, Ret	149
15-4	Colt Lightweight commander .45 ACP	150
15-5	Engraved Colt Commander .45 ACP	150
15-6	Photograph–Texas Ranger, Joaquin Jackson, Ret.	151
15-7	Colt Lightweight Defender . 45 ACP	151
15-8	FTRA membership certificate	152
16-1	Photo Captains Hamer and Stevens	158
16-2	Captains Stevens & Hamer, S&W .32 model 1903 revolver	159
16-3	Photo Captain/Chaplain Pierre Bernard Hill	159
16-4	Texas Ranger prayer from Stan Guffey memorial program	160
16-5	Browning Renaissance 9mm high power	160
16-6	Photo Ranger Aycock/author with Winchester trapper carbine	161
16-7	M1, 30 caliber carbine owned by Texas Ranger Sgt. John Aycock, Retired	161
16-8	Close up of Ranger Aycock's personalized carbine stock	162
16-9	Colt python of late H. Joaquin Jackson	162
16-10	photo of late H. Joaquin Jackson and author	163
16-11	H. Joaquin Jackson commemorative Bowie Knife	163
16-12	2 Leather Texas Ranger Belt sets (John Aycock)	164
16-13	2 Leather Texas Ranger Belt sets (Milton Wright)	164
17-1	S&W .38 Model 10, documented to 3 Rangers	168
17-2	Pair Model 19 S&Ws document to Capt. G. W. Burks	168
17-3	S&W Model 19 Texas Ranger Commemorative documented to Capt Butch Albers	169
17-4	Sig Sauer P220 documented to Lt. Joe Hutson	169
17-5	Sig Sauer P226 document to Sgt Ronnie Griffith	170
17-6	Special Texas Ranger Edition Beretta M92, Lt Bob Favor	170
17-7	Colt Lightweight Commander .45 ACP, Ed Gooding	171
17-8	Colt 1911A1 customized, documented to Sgt. Kyle Dean	171
17-9	Colt 1911A1 concealed carry officers (CCO) Sgt Steve Boyd	172

17-10	1911A1 Argentine Colt, engraved and owned by Sgt Doyle Holdridge	172
17-11	Glock Model 33 documented to Major Shawn Palmer (ret)	173
17-12	Para Ordinance 1911 .45 ACP high capacity Major Jeff Collins	174
17-13	Colt Lightweight Commander .45 ACP, Lt Chris Clark	174
17-14	Colt Lightweight Defender .45 ACP, Sgt Mike Smith	175
17-15	Sturm Ruger Mini-14, DPS issue, Sgt Steve Foster	175
17-16	Winchester Model 1892 trapper, 44/40, Sgt Ronald Stewart	176
17-17	Colt combat commander, stainless, Cogan Custom, Capt. Jack Dean	177
17-18	Colt Gold Cup National Match, Sgt Jim Huggins	177
18-1	Early 8 Reales Ranger badge	184
18-2	Early highway patrol badge, circa 1935	185
18-3	Two nonstandard Ranger badges	186
18-4	Three authorized DPS Texas Ranger badges	186
18-5	Grouping of five Texas Ranger Cinco peso badges	187
18-6	Gold Captains badge & documentation Bob Mitchell	188
18-7	Two Former Texas Ranger Foundation badges, one Schreiner III badge	189
18-8	Badge & rubber mold, Gatesville prison	189
18-9	Close up of badge mold, Gatesville prison	190
18-10	75th Anniversary badge	191
18-11	Two Texas prison system correctional officer badges	192
18-12	Two sets early vintage handcuffs	192
18-13	Two modern era handcuff sets	193
18-14	Engraved set of Colt handcuffs	193
18-15	Leg or ankle restraints	194

CHAPTER 1

ARMS OF THE COLONY

Many historians accept that the Texas Rangers date back to the colonizing years of Stephen F. Austin. Their formation is tied to the year 1823. These citizen soldiers were neither organized nor law men. Contemporary records suggest that 1835 was the date for their formation. In either case these brave volunteer citizen soldiers protected Texas frontier settlements from hostile Comanche and Kiowa Indians from north of the Red River. The Comanche, known as Lords of the Plains, proved to be the fiercest of all hostile tribes. They were first to use the horse. Mounted they had an advantage over their enemies. Some refer to this period in Ranger history as the time of the citizen soldier. During the years of the Republic of Texas 1835 to 1845, these citizen soldiers also gathered to fend off both bandits and military incursions from Mexico. Neither of these invaders accepted Texas independence. Regardless of designation, Ranger companies displayed like characteristics. They volunteered to serve a specific time, usually three to six months. They wore no uniform, carried no flag, and they furnished their own arms and horses. During the 1823 timeframe, in the time of the Austin Colony, approximately ten men were recruited to serve as Rangers to defeat a band of hostile Indians.

1835 was the official year that the interim government authorized the corps of Texas Rangers. Exactly what firearms were these Rangers carrying?

We know from history and contemporary accounts that they carried a variety of flintlock pistols and rifles. They were known as a flintlock due to the method of firing the black powder. A lock mechanism induced a spark when a piece of flint located on the hammer contacted the metal striker near the pan. Primed powder in the pan ignited a spark that traveled through a drilled channel in the breech. This spark ignited the packed powder charge and projectile in the interior rear of the barrel. Projectiles used in these weapons ranged from lead pellets to broken glass, nails and as a last resort small rock chips. Many of the early Texas flintlocks were carried west from such manufacturing areas as Pennsylvania, Kentucky and even the eastern seaboard. The most common and versatile of these was the smooth bore shotgun. With the scarcity of available weapons the shotgun was the most versatility and the most utilized. It could be loaded with lead shot for small game and larger projectiles for more serious shooting. As mentioned before if an early pioneer shooter could choose one weapon, it was the shotgun. Almost as important as a self defense tool, it was a means to put meat on the table. The hunting of wild game was vital to early survival. Also popular at the time was the Hawkin rifle, manufactured by the Hawkin Brothers of St. Louis, Missouri circa 1820's. Kentucky and Plains rifles were also well represented. One well known maker of these was S. Odell of Natchez, Mississippi. Both types were known for their ruggedness and accuracy. Some of the early eastern gun makers whose firearms showed up on the Texas frontier were such names as Turner Rifles, John H. Hall, and Horace Dimick to name a few. Also popular were the United States issued military pistols and rifles. Some were kept from militia service and others bought from surplus stocks. And then there were some that were merely misappropriated. The common calibers for the single shot flintlock pistols were .54 and .69 calibers. The model 1826 US Army issue flintlock pistol was produced by such well known makers as W. Evans, Asa Waters and Robert Johnson. These makers also shared later contracts for the 1836 and 1842 U.S. model pistols. Another popular single shot pistol was the 1826 flintlock Navy made by Simeon North of Middleton, Connecticut. A later change over from flintlock to percussion cap ignition system occurred on the commercial market around the late 1830's. This resulted in the alterations of pistols from the manufacturers Asa Waters and Robert Johnson. These converted pistols utilizing the percussion cap system proved highly dependable. The US model 1842 single shot percussion pistol by Henry Aston of Middleton, Connecticut saw wide use not only in the Mexican war of 1846 but later as a peace keeper on the Texas frontier. One early lock maker who specialized in producing replacement flintlock to percussion lock assemblies was G. Goulcher, New York, NY. He manufactured replacement lock assemblies from 1853 to 1872.

Let us not forget the importance of the early muskets. The US model 1840 flintlock in .69 caliber saw wide use. It was replaced by the improved percussion fired US model 1841 and 1842 muskets. Most of these were made at the US government arsenal located at Harpers Ferry, Virginia and were in use for many years. The list of the United States government contract musket makers is to lengthy to mention. Early Texas Republic settlers were also known to carry acquired Mexican army issued muskets. Some of these include the British .61 caliber Baker rifle, however, the .75 caliber East India pattern Brown Bess was the most numerous. This was the standard arm of the Mexican army. It was also used by the Texan defenders at the Alamo. Mexican officer Jose Enrique De La Pena reported that every man in the Alamo had 3 or 4 of these muskets stacked up for their use. The French army Charleville rifle was another military musket that in later years saw popular service. Many of these, after years of French occupation and colonization, fell into civilian hands. We will never completely know the vast extent of the weapons used at the battle of the Alamo. A Mexican army's inventory list from April 1836 listed a total of 816 muskets, 21 cannon and 14,600 cartridges that were captured and sent back to Mexico. Most of these were captured at the siege of Bexar.

Flintlock rifles and pistols as well as their upgraded percussion ignition system replacements were used on the Texas frontier long after their time of obsolescence. Due to their geographical isolation to the eastern manufacturing areas early Texans had by necessity to maintain these outdated weapons in a constant state of readiness. This was a matter of survival to defend against hostile Comanche and Kiowa warriors. Indian warriors rarely carried firearms. Their main threat came from their skill with a bow and arrow. Many times they outperformed the single shot muskets. It could take two or more minutes for a Texas frontiersman to reload their single shot rifles. An Indian warrior could hurl 5 or more arrows in this period of time. Hostiles learned to wait until the Texans fired their loaded single shot muskets to stage their charge. Seasoned frontiersmen carried multiple pistols and at least one rifle or shotgun. This multiple selection helped make up for their single shot limitation. When all else failed a trusted Bowie type knife could save the day. No self respecting Ranger would be caught on scout without his Bowie knife. It was probably the most utilized of all his kit, from an eating utensil to skinning and preparing wild game to such ordained tasks of personal hygiene as an occasional shave. To make a point, Texas Ranger Robert Hall who joined a company mustered by Ben McCulloch in the final days of the republic spent $25.00 for the finest Bowie knife he could buy. He knew the Mexican "Rancheros, the irregular equivalent of Mustang Grays "cow-boys" fought with lariats. As a matter of clarification the Mustang Grays were a company of Rangers from Corpus Christi under the command of Captain Mabry B. Gray. He led a controversial unit that sometimes was difficult to determine which side his loyalties were on. The mounted rancheros roped an enemy around the neck and dragging him until he choked to death. A good Bowie knife could free a Ranger from this predicament. Even during this early time period the long sword was becoming merely ceremonial. It was rarely used as an offensive weapon. It was being relegated to serve as a symbol of the Officer Corps and to rally troops into battle. Percussion weapons though obsolete by the late 1860's were used far into the late 19th century.

CHAPTER 1

ILLUSTRATIONS

1-1 Plains rifle: Early example of a plains type rifle .54 caliber, rifled bull barrel circa 1820. Originally flintlock but converted to percussion circa 1860s. Replacement lock marked "G.GOUCHER, New York, N.Y."(Author's collection)

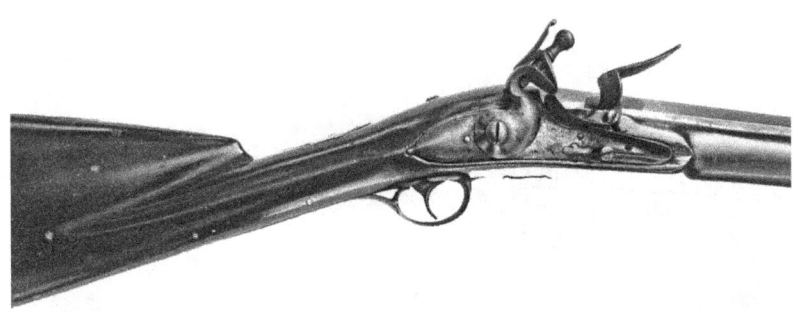

1-2 Early flintlock fowling piece: Example of early American flintlock "Long Tom" shotgun made circa 1780. Type often seen on the early frontier. Barrel length 60.2 inches overall length 76 inches. Photo cropped to highlight lock mechanism. (Bobby Vance collection)

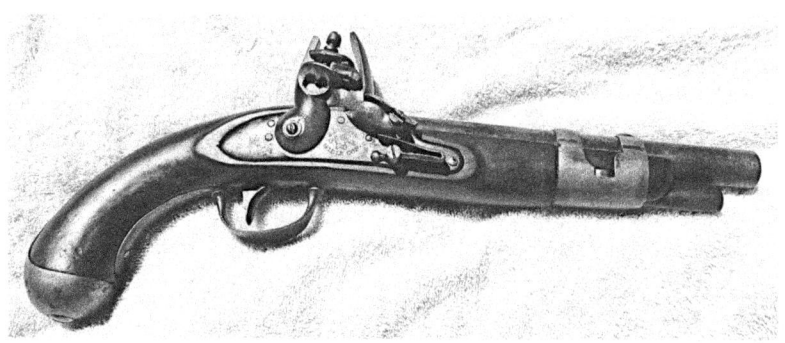

1-3 US Model 1816 flintlock pistol: Smooth bore .54 caliber, U.S. issue, lock marked "S. North Middleton, Conn" mfg circa 1817. (Author's collection)

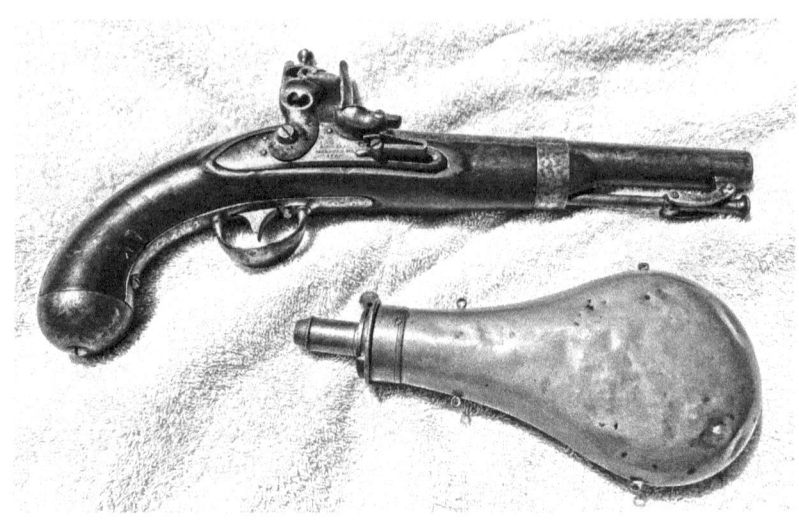

1-4 US Model 1836 flintlock pistol: Smooth bore .54 caliber, U.S. issue, lock marked "A.Waters, Millbury, MS, 1837," top of barrel marked U.S. (Author's collection)

1-5 Bowie knife: Example of Bowie style hunting knife commonly carried on the frontier. Named after James Bowie who made it famous. Bowie died in 1836 defending the Alamo.

CHAPTER 2

ARMING THE REPUBLIC

In the year 1835 the Texas Rangers were officially established by the interim government of Texas. It authorized three companies of 56 men each. These companies were headed by a Captain and aided by a 1st and 2nd Lieutenant. Robert M. Williamson served as Major and directed operations of the companies. The first 3 elected Captains were Isaac Burton, William Arrington and John T. Tumlinson. Privates who signed on for one year were paid $1.25 per day. Each Ranger was required to furnish his own arms, ammunition and mounts. The majority of weapons carried by the early Rangers were flintlock and percussion fired muskets and pistols. Many of these were the type mentioned in chapter one. Individual weapons were scarce and highly prized by the frontier settlers. Hostile Comanche Indians were sometimes armed with firearms taken during raids on the early pioneers. The mere possession of these weapons however was not the threat it might suggest. Early Native American tribes lacked the supply support system to render these weapons effective. Availability of black powder shot and replacement parts were a major challenge. As the number of frontier settlers increased access to sutler supplies became more prevalent. The Indian bow and arrow and lance remained the main armament for Comanche and Kiowa warriors. Even with these primitive weapons hostile Indians remained a constant and deadly threat. Early settlers lived in constant fear of a surprise Indian attack. As we discussed in chapter one the first company of Rangers were formed to combat this problem.

As the Republic became more organized small purchases were allocated for the acquisition of firearms. State funds were always a challenge for the new republic. There was never enough money. One of the most notable arms purchases made by the Republic was in August 1839. A total sale of 180 Colt Patterson Model 1839 revolving carbines and 180 holster pistols were contracted with the Patterson Arms Company of Patterson, New Jersey. These Colt arms were distributed by E. W. Moore, Commodore of the Texas Fleet and were to be dedicated to the vessels of war. 180 carbines with bullet molds were agreed to be delivered at $55.00 each. Also agreed was the delivery of 180 belt pistols with 8 inch barrels at $35.00 each with levers and bullet molds. Also included were 180 cap primers which would work for both carbines and pistols at $1.50 each. This order reached Galveston, Texas in early November 1839.

When President Sam Houston disbanded the Texas Navy, a quantity of model No. 5 Paterson holster pistols were passed down to the Texas Rangers. The main reciprocate of these revolvers was Captain John Coffee "Jack" Hayes. John C. Hayes, know in Texas as Jack Hayes, was born on January 28, 1817 in Wilson County, Tennessee. He came from the same part of the country as Sam Houston, Andrew Jackson and McCullochs. Hayes came to Texas in 1837 and took up residence in San Antonio. Accounts say that he joined the Texas Rangers and fought Indians and Mexicans under Deaf Smith and Henry W. Karnes. He equipped his Rangers with this Colt five shot .36 caliber revolving pistol. Little did he know that with it he would change the entire course of how battles on the frontier would be fought. The battle we call "Hayes Big Fight" also known as the "Battle of Walker Creek" took place June 8, 1844. Texas Ranger Captain John C. Hayes and 15 of his Rangers engaged a far superi-or number of 70–80 hostile Indians. Captain Hayes and his Rangers armed with the 5 shot Paterson revolvers attacked the hostiles on their own ground killing and wounding more than half their num-ber. Word of the phenomenal performance of these Colt revolvers quickly spread. The year 1844 was also paramount to firearms development as it was the year the United States military service officially replaced the flintlock arms with those of the percussion system. Although the Colt Paterson was revolutionary for its time it was not without its shortcomings. It still however, remained the best weapon available. It would be several years before Colt's pis-tols would be common place among either frontier citizens or Texas Rangers. Visionaries such as Samuel Walker were already planning improvements for a heavier caliber revolver. This will lead to the production of what will become the Colt Walker revolving pistol. The Walker Colt was named after Samuel H. Walker, Texas Rang-er and later Captain of the United States Mounted Rifles. Samuel Walker was born in the town Toaping Castle, Prince George Coun-ty, Maryland 24 February 1817. He migrated to Texas in 1842 and joined Captain Jesse Billingsleys Company of mounted volunteers. Over the next four years Captain Walker's vast knowledge of tactics and frontier fighting led him to contact Samuel Colt in 1846. This event resulted in Colt's return to gun making only four years after the Paterson enterprise collapsed.

The fledgling Paterson Arms Company founded by Sam Colt came to have high regard for the great Republic of Texas and for the courageous Rangers who in turn were using their Colt firearms. The later Dragoon models bore cylinder scenes depicting the routing of some 70-80 Comanche by the Texas Rangers. The No. 5 Paterson holster pistols were identified as the "Texas Model" and Colt himself referred to this model by this name. During this time period Colt did their best to sell revolving arms to Texas. The Republic and its fighting men did more to foster the sale of Colt arms than the United States or any other customer. In 1845 Texas was annexed and became a part of the United States. In this year the availability of federally provided firearms increased. These US issued firearms were highly effective in the hands of Texans leading up to the formal declaration of the Mexican war. Prior to this declaration there was an undeclared war with General Santa Ana and the Mexican army over the disputed area between the Rio Grande and the Nueces

River. This area was known as the Nueces Strip. Just as challenging to the Texas settlers were bandit depreciations.

The first Congress of the Republic of Texas had passed the boundary act attempting to establish the permanent border. The Sabine and Red rivers were fixed as the northern border between Texas and the United states with the entire Rio Grande being the southwestern and western borders. This encompassed the so called Nueces Strip to the south. Mexico never accepted the Rio Grande as the southern border which they felt should be the Nueces River. It is this thinking that led to numerous incursions and minor conflicts between Mexican nationals and frontier Texans. This disputed area remained a hot spot far up into the 20th century. It would lead the newly annexed state of Texas into the Mexican war in 1846.

CHAPTER 2

ILLUSTRATIONS

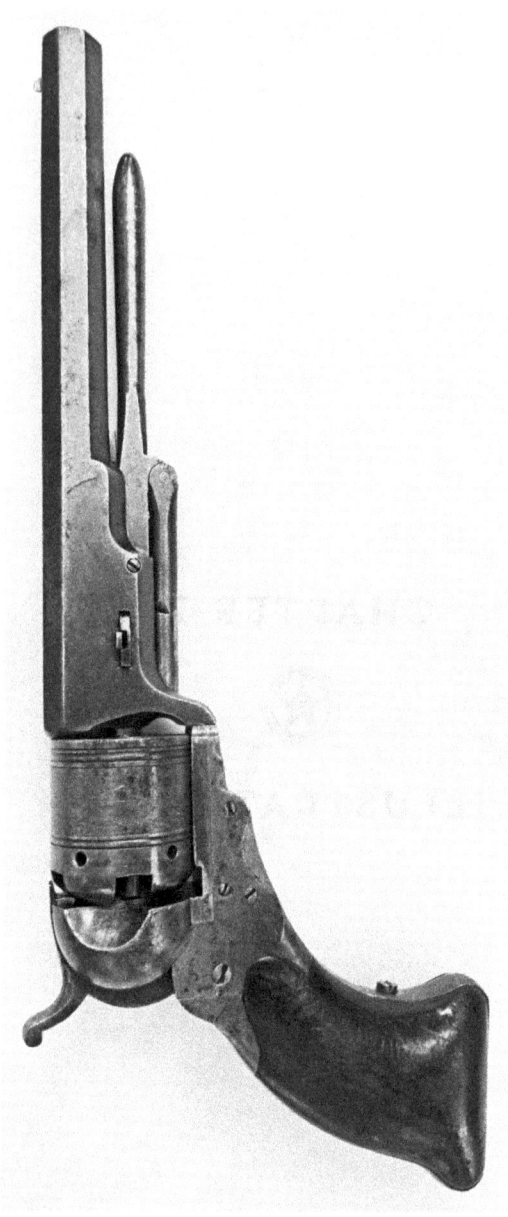

2-1 Paterson Colt: Paterson Colt No. 5 holster pistol, .36 caliber, 5 shot percussion. So popular in Texas that it was referred to as the "Texas Model." This later example has the loading lever. (Bobby Vance collection)

2-2 Paterson Colt remake: Example of a European remake of the No. 5 Paterson revolver. 36 caliber, 5 shot circa 1850's, military flap holster circa 1860's The Paterson No 5 was so popular that it was copied and imported. This example came out of Mexico. (Author's collection)

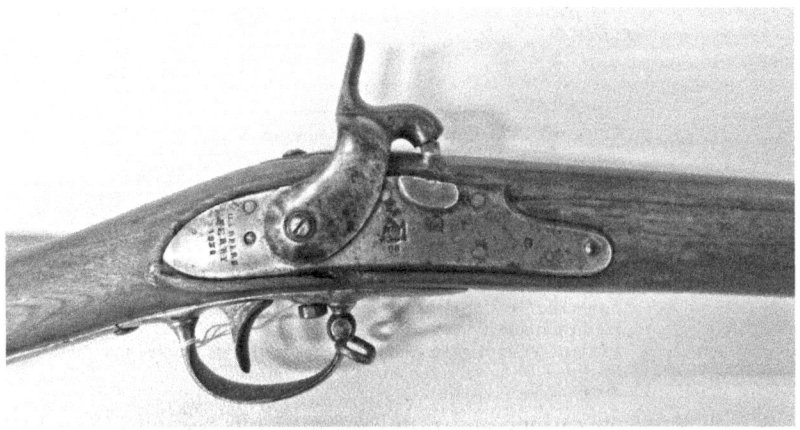

2-3 U.S. Model 1816 musket: Originally flintlock and later converted to percussion, produced 1816–1844. Largest production total of all U.S. muskets with over 325,000 made. (Author's collection)

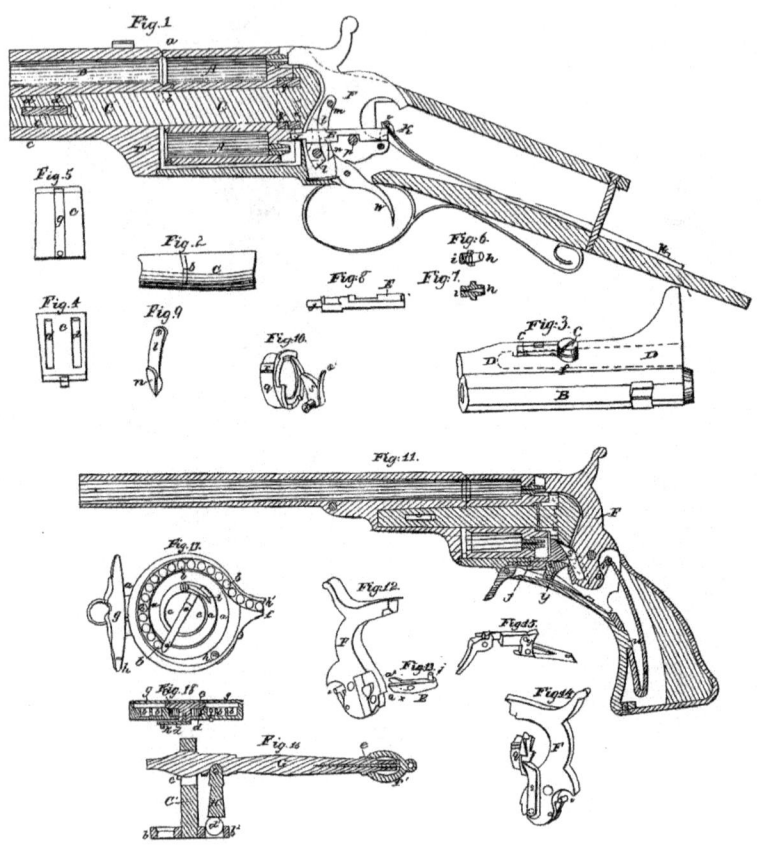

Colt's second U.S. patent, No. 1304, issued August 29th 1839, and depicting the Model 1839 Carbine (without attached loading lever) and the No. 5 Holster or Texas Paterson pistol (also without attached lever). These pictures make quite clear the operation of the Model 1839 type longarms and the production Paterson revolving pistols, as well as the combination powder and ball flasks, the cap primer, bullet mold, and the loading lever-combination wrench-screwdriver-nipple pick. Nine specific claims were listed by Colt in this important patent document: "1. The making of a groove or channel on the arbor . . . for the purpose of conducting off the smoke from the lateral discharge, and thus preserving the arbor clean within the receiver, and the tube by which the barrel is connected.

2-4 Colt Paterson carbine and pistol patent: Colts second U.S. patent depicting the 1839 revolving carbine and No. 5 holster or Texas Paterson pistol (public record).

CHAPTER 3

WAR WITH MEXICO

Conflicts with Mexico haunted Texas settlers and were a constant threat to the stability of the Republic. The disputed area known as the Nueces Strip between the Rio Grande and Nueces rivers remained a festering wound to both Mexico and the Texas Republic. The situation did not improve with the annexation to the United States in 1845. In March 1842 the Mexican general Rafael Vasquez invaded Texas and occupied San Antonio. The city was largely deserted because Texas Rangers had shadowed the invading force. General Vasquez freed three of Captain Hayes' Rangers whom he had captured and then headed back to Mexico. San Antonio was again attached and occupied until September 20, 1842 by a large expeditionary force under General Woll. He headed back to Mexico shortly after the 20th.

In preparing for an all out war, Texas banded together to form the first Texas Mounted Rifles as part of the states quota for federal service. Jack Hayes was named Colonel and Sam Walker Lieutenant Colonel. Seven of the ten companies were Rangers. The unit contained so many former Rangers that it remained essentially a Ranger unit. Weapons carried by these Rangers/soldiers appear to be a mixture of personal property and arms and equipment drawn from U.S. ordnance officers. In Walkers case, it included Colts Revolvers. When mustered into federal service Captain Hayes drew as many revolvers as he could get his hands on; a total of 32 in all. He issued these to his men. Besides the Colt revolvers a list of Ranger weaponry as provided by Walker at Matamoros on July 22, 1846 is as follows:

- 9   Colts revolving carbines
- 3   contract brown full stock rifles
- 6   Halls carbines
- 9   carbine or rifle cartridge boxes
- 3   military waist belts
- 7   military belt plates
- 4   Colts bullet molds
- 3   military pistol flasks
- 3   Colt wrenches and screwdrivers
- 2   rifle wipers
- 4   capper flasks
- 5   rifle pouches

Sam Walker would move from the Ranger force to an appointment as a Captain of Mounted Rifles in the regular U.S. Army. The United States forces during the Mexican conflict were initially led by General Zachary Taylor. For nine months in the summer of 1845, he gathered troops on the disputed ground of the Nueces Strip. He moved south opposite Matamoros where he prepared for war. He mustered several companies of Hayes Rangers into federal service. It was during this time that 60 of General Taylor's dragoons were captured while on scout on the Rio Grande. Taylor asked the Governor of Texas for 4 regiments, 2 mounted, 2 foot. This was the call to fight that the Texans had longed for. It escalated from here.

    Despite the success of the original Colt revolvers in Texas the United States government showed no interest in the weapon. Many higher ranking officers in the regular United States military were traditional in their opinions on military weapons with multiple shot capabilities. The philosophy of these old line conventional military thinkers was that giving a soldier the capability to fire multiple shots in rapid succession would lead to a waste of ammunition. Whether they were concerned with the logistics of resupply or simply the cost, it was a line of thinking which limited the full capability of the Army for many years.. This logic contributed to the difficulties that Colt encountered with military sales. This eventually, in part, led Colt into receivership in 1842, prompting Walker and Colt to design a new and improved upscale revolver. Together Walker and Colt worked out specifications and tooling for the new pistol, production began in January 1847. It was a .44 caliber 6 shot weapon that at 4 lb 9 oz was Colts heaviest production revolver. Primarily issued to the Texas Rangers it was formally designated the Walker Model. Its introduction during the Mexican war insured Colt's future success. Approximately 1100 were manufactured in 1847. Captain Walker convinced the United States to purchase 1000 of the pistols. Due to its excessive weight, the Walker Colt was designed to be carried in a dual holster brace mounted on the saddle. The Walker is the greatest prize of any Colt collection as slightly more than 10% survived. Two Walker model Colts were presented to Captain Walker by Samuel Colt and shipped to Mexico in late July 1847. Four days later Captain Walker met his death leading a charge in the streets of Huamantla, Tiaxeala, Mexico. This violent battle involved over 500 of General Santa Anna's lancers supported by artillery. Captain Walker's Colts were found on his body completely empty attesting to his valiant fight right to the very end. The fame of the Walker Colts led to the immediate production in 1848 of Samuel Colt's next model known as the First Model Dragoon. Captain Walker's death was quite a loss to the federal army for which he was serving and also to the state of Texas. John Coffee Hayes kept up the battle with increased vengeance.

Hayes arrived in Vera Cruz on October 17, 1848. Two days later the first consignment of Colts Walker Model revolvers were delivered and issued to the Texas Rangers. As mentioned before, the most common weapons carried by United States forces and supporting Rangers, were the government arsenal provided muskets and pistols. This included the U.S. model 1841 in 1842 percussion muskets in .54 caliber. Also known as the "Mississippi Rifle" made at Harpers Ferry arsenal and the US model 1842 percussion musket in .69 caliber. The 1842 musket was made at the Springfield and Harpers Ferry arsenals. Their production totaled over 275,000. The commonly used primary military single shot pistol was the US model 1842 percussion pistol. It was made by Henry Aston and Ira Johnson of Middleton, Connecticut. Although the war was nearing end Captain John C. Hayes was actively involved in the conflict. He overcame stiff Mexican resistance of Puebla. He broke through and cleared a path all the way to Mexico City. The Mexican war secured Mexican recognition of Texas as part of the United States with the Rio Grande as its southwestern boundary. The war was costly. Great Rangers like Walker and Gillespie were dead. Less noble Rangers gave the service a tarnished reputation for brutality that lingered for many years. But the fame of the Ranger force spread beyond the boundaries of Texas. The Texas Rangers were becoming a legend.

CHAPTER 3

ILLUSTRATIONS

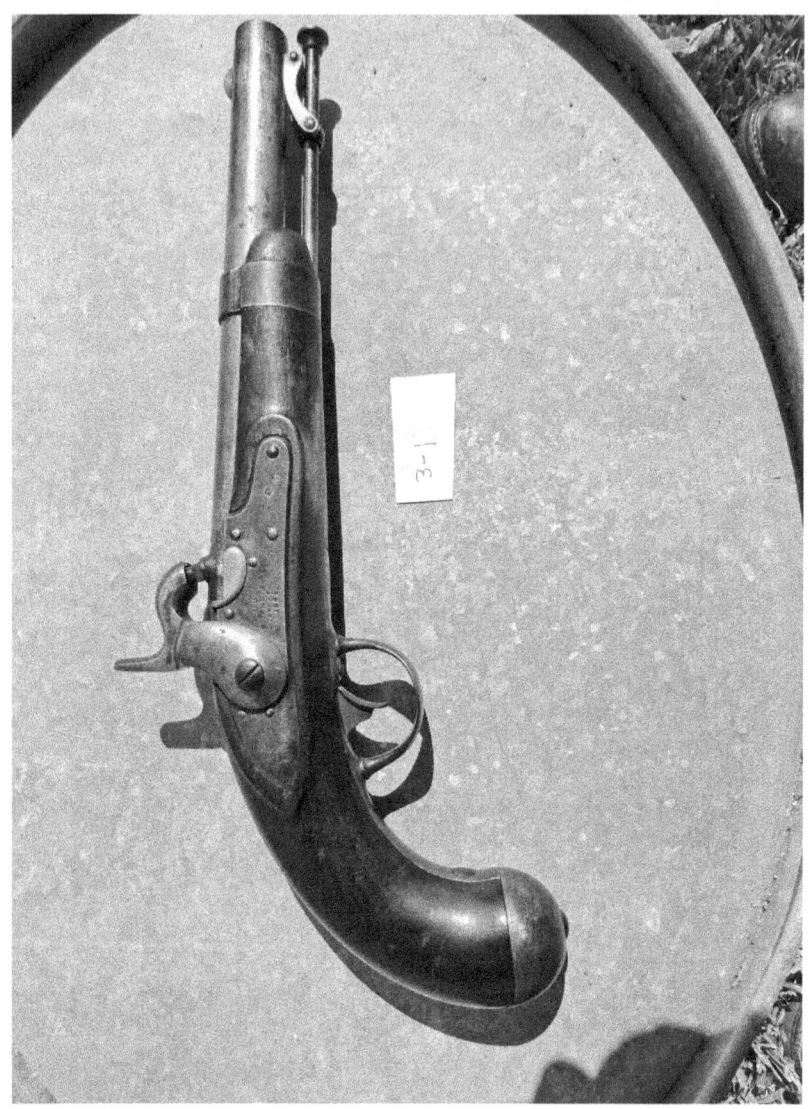

3-1 U.S. Model 1836 flintlock pistol. .54 caliber, smooth bore, single shot pistol. U.S. Army issue mfg by R. Johnson of Middleton, Conn circa 1844. Originally flintlock and later arsenal converted to percussion. (Author's collection)

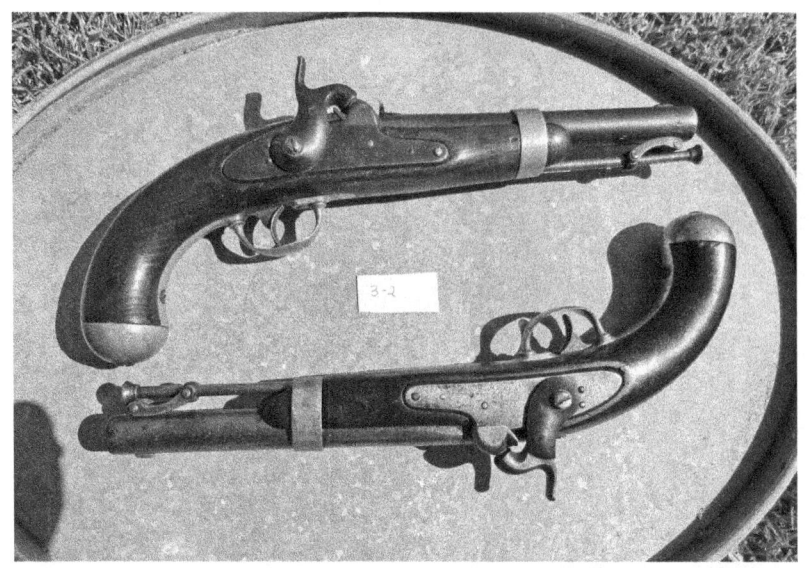

3-2 U.S. Model 1842 percussion pistol: Pictured are two examples of the U.S. Army .54 caliber, smooth bore pistol. *Top*–example mfg in 1850 by H. Aston, Midddleton, Conn. *Bottom*–example mfg 1853 by I. N. Johnson of Middleton, Conn. (Author's collection)

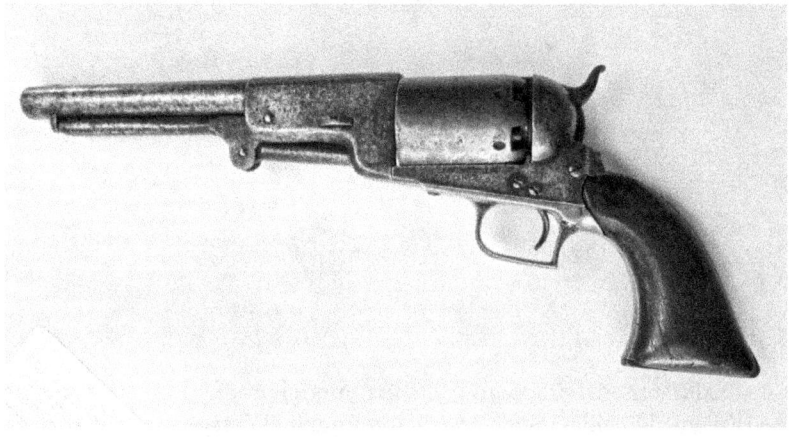

3-3 Walker Colt: The Walker is the prize of any collection with less than 10% survival rate, .44 caliber, six shot , with 9 inch barrel, weighing 4 lb 9 oz , it was Colts largest pistol. Example mfg 1847 and is marked "C Company." (Bobby Vance collection)

3-4 U.S. First model dragoon: Colts first model production revolver after the Walker. .44 caliber, with 7 ½' half round, half octagon barrel. Slightly lighter than the Walker, it had numerous improvements. This example mfg 1848. (Author's collection)

CHAPTER 4

THE TIME BETWEEN THE WARS

Soldiers, Rangers and civilian volunteers returning to life after the Mexican war found a time of short supplies, continued bandit raids and the constant conflict with hostile Indians. During the 1850's to 1861 the firearms industry made many advances. Nothing to compare with the 1862-65 era but still some important advances in firearms technology occurred. Although not through a government contract, Colt was able to market many of his pistols to the civilian buyer. During the early 1850's the Colt pocket model 1849 revolver became popular. Called the pocket model because of its moderate size, it was designed to be carried in a coat pocket. Production began in 1850. It was a .31 caliber, 5 shot percussion revolver. It was available in limited numbers to the private buyers. It was called the California Gold Rush Model. It was popular in the early gold fields in California. Its numbers were well represented in Texas as well as other parts of the country. Over 325,000 Hartford models were sold. Even more popular to the private buyer was the larger .36 caliber percussion Navy revolver. It was marketed in 1851 and continued into the 1870's. It was very popular to the civilian market and at the commencement of the Civil War became one of the primary issued Union Army service revolvers. A total of 215,000 were produced at Hartford, Connecticut. It was Colts primary medium frame revolver during the percussion period. Also available on the civilian market was the Colt Model 1855 (Root Model) side hammer revolver in .28 caliber. It entered into production in 1855. It was the design that prompted the development and marketing of the 1855 Model Revolving Carbine and Rifle. Not to forget other manufacturers, the Whitney Navy and Eagle Company revolver produced in the 1850's had a total quantity of 33,000. It was a .36 caliber, 6 shot single action revolver. The Whitney Navy is one of the first practical solid frame revolvers and was an early competitor to the Colt. The Eli Whitney Company of New Haven, Connecticut, was the first to manufacture the initial Walker Model Colts. Later Colt took over production on their own. Just for clarification, the Whitney Firearms Company was founded by Eli Whitney most known for his invention of the cotton gin. Another Colt competitor was the Remington Arms Company of Ilion, New York. It produced a number of pocket revolvers in the late 1850's, such as the Remington/Beals first, second and third model pocket revolver in .31 caliber. Christian Sharps and Company and Sharps and Hankins of Philadelphia marketed a 4 shot pepper box in .22, .30 and.32 calibers in the year 1859. It was very popular and well utilized as a gamblers gun for up close protection. Allen and Wheelock marketed a large frame revolver in .34 caliber in 1857. They also marketed the .34 caliber 5 barrel pepper box pistol. It was so named because the arrangement of barrels resembled the top of a pepper shaker. There were other limited production firearms on the frontier as well as Belgium and English export weapons. For the sake of brevity we will stop with these.

Even though there were a relatively large total of varied firearms available, the logistics of resupply of these weapons was simple. All used bulk black powder and most used standard sized percussion caps. Both were readily available on the Texas frontier. Projectiles were most commonly lead ball ammunition that the user could self produce. They made their own bullets by melting lead block and pouring the lead into a commercial bullet mold. When the lead cooled it received a rough polish and was ready to start the loading process. Black powder in a measured amount was poured into the barrel, the lead ball wrapped in cotton swab was packed in the barrel with a rammer, a percussion cap was attached to the breech nipple and it was ready to fire. No need for manufactured self contained ammunition that would become popular much later in the late 1860's.

With all the varied types of revolvers and pepper box pistols available on the civilian market, it still took money and an accessibility to acquire firearms from a retailer. It was easy for a customer on the east coast with their readily available markets. It was another thing for those on the Texas frontier. Most settlers lived an isolated life. Money was hard to come by and even if available it was difficult to access a nearby firearms retailer which was few and far apart. Such major shipping centers as El Paso, San Antonio, Galveston and Austin stocked many of the supplies and firearms needed in the less populated areas. Eager entrepreneurs willing to risk theft from bandits or hostile Indians would purchase supplies from these major hubs and transport them by wagons to less accessible areas.

Hostile Indians such as the renegade Seminole Chieftain Coacoochee, better known as Wild Cat, kept violence a major concern on the Mexican border. By 1855, Texas frontiersmen were well acquainted with Wild Cat. A group of James H. Callahan's Rangers and those of Captain William R. Henry crossed the Rio Grande four miles from Eagle Pass and entered Mexico. They were determined to fight Wild Cat, his Indian warriors, Black Seminoles, Mexican regulars or anyone else. The Mounted Rangers moved beyond the sand hills and hugged the river banks. At a point some twenty miles into Mexico the Rangers came under fire from Mexican regulars and Indian scouts of which Wild Cat was believed to be a member. A group numbering some 700 swarmed out of the thickets. Pistols, rifles and shotguns rang out on every side. A desperate battle ensued. Estimates vary as to the number killed or wounded but it seems they were less than would be expected. Callahan retreated to the border at Piedras Negras, then a settlement of approximately 1,500 inhabitants. The Alcalde surrendered the town and its arsenal. The arsenal was said to constitute quite a military museum. When a sizable Mexican force approached Callahan's position, he set fires that resulted in the burning of the town and caused him to cross back into Texas. Callahan's reckless incursions stirred up old embers of hatred, fear and mistrust along the border. The reason I motioned Callahan's raid is to set the tone of the time along the border.

Even though the Mexican war was over, there were still active hostilities between Texans and Mexican nationals. To Anglo Texans Callahan and his men were freedom fighters and brave defenders of the border. To those of Mexican heritage, on both sides of the river, the Texans were nothing more than soldiers of fortune and privateers. Rangers were seen to be riders from hell. So what happened to the weapons seized in Piedras Negras? They went to arm Texas frontiersman who boldly planned to use them on another incursion. A good dependable firearm as we discussed was of the utmost value and importance even some of the antiquated arms seized in their raids.

The average Ranger was usually a cash poor individual. Although of good character they lacked the finer necessaries of their frontier counterparts. If a Ranger owned a good horse, rifle and hand gun he was said to be in "high cotton." This is one of the reasons the Rangers took such good care of their weapons and horses. These were their prized possessions and sometimes the only means of personal survival. It always amazed me when I watch a modern day motion picture where the western hero after a shoot out, rides off leaving the outlaw and his weapons on the ground. This would never happen. An early Ranger would no more abandon a rifle or pistol than they would a sack of gold. A good pistol at this time period more than not was more valuable than the person that carried it. Human life was cheap and it took devoted Rangers to enforce the peace and give meaning to law and order. It has been said that the early Texas Rangers were rough, hard core, dangerous men. Well, it took this type of individual to tame the savage land that was Texas in the 1850's. With virtually no formal established law in many remote communities, it was the Rangers and the rule of the gun that kept a resemblance of order. It was a rough untamed country that required rough men to protect it. They were at many times the only thing between life and death on the southern and western frontiers of Texas.

CHAPTER 4

ILLUSTRATIONS

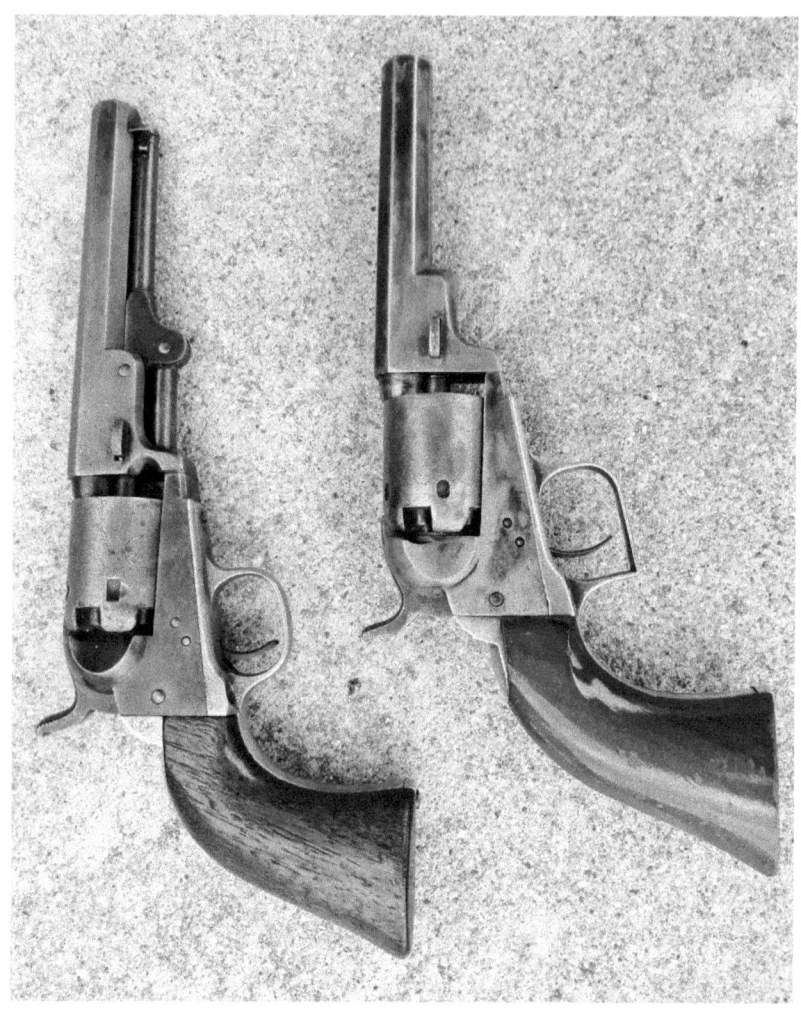

4-1 Colt Model 1849 pocket: *Left* – this model was widely used and marketed well for Colt. A five shot .31 caliber revolver, it came in numerous variations. *Right* – for size comparison is a Baby Dragoon mfg in 1848 which was the forerunner to the pocket models. (Authors collection)

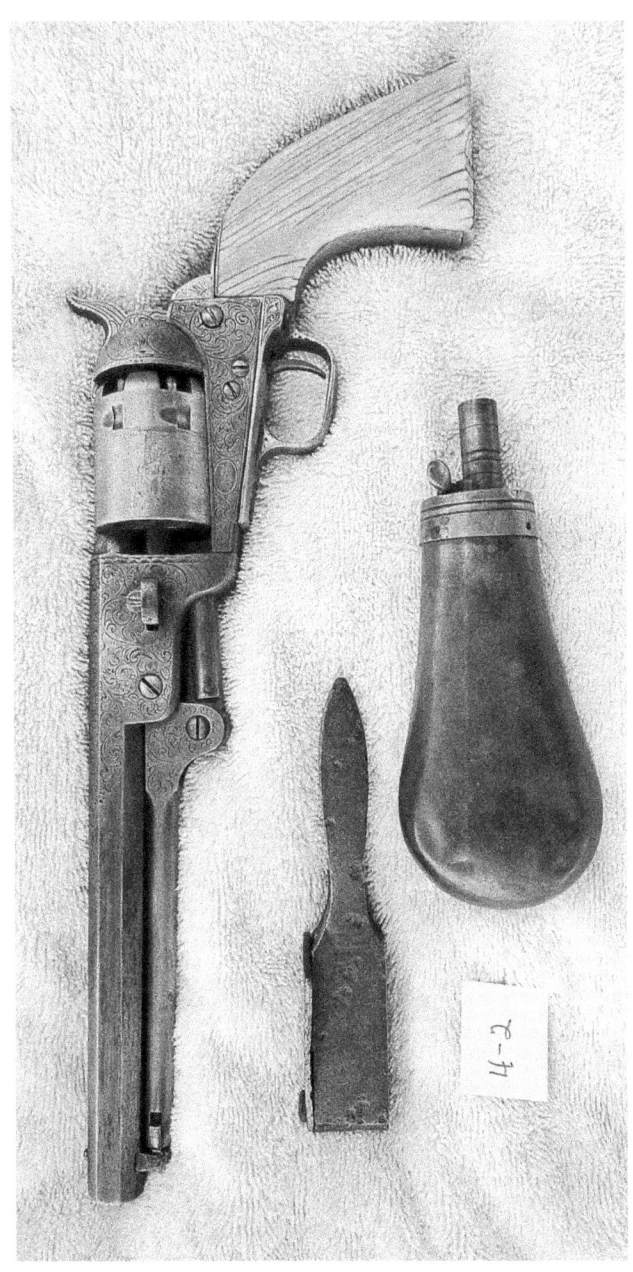

4-2 Colt Model Navy 1851: .36 caliber, 6 shot single action revolver. Example has period engraving and one piece ivory grips, mfg in early 1857. (Author's collection)

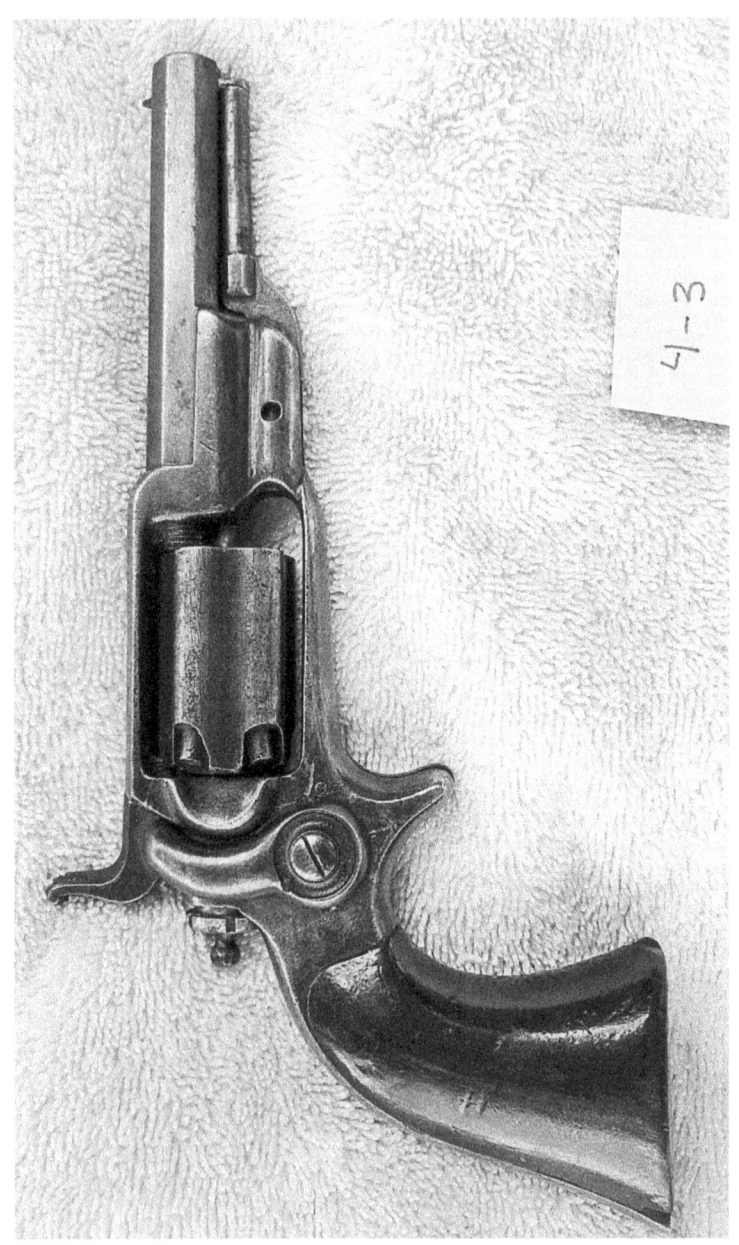

4-3 Colt Root revolver: Side hammer, 6 shot, .28 caliber, single action revolver, first marketed in 1855. This example was mfg in 1861. (Author's collection)

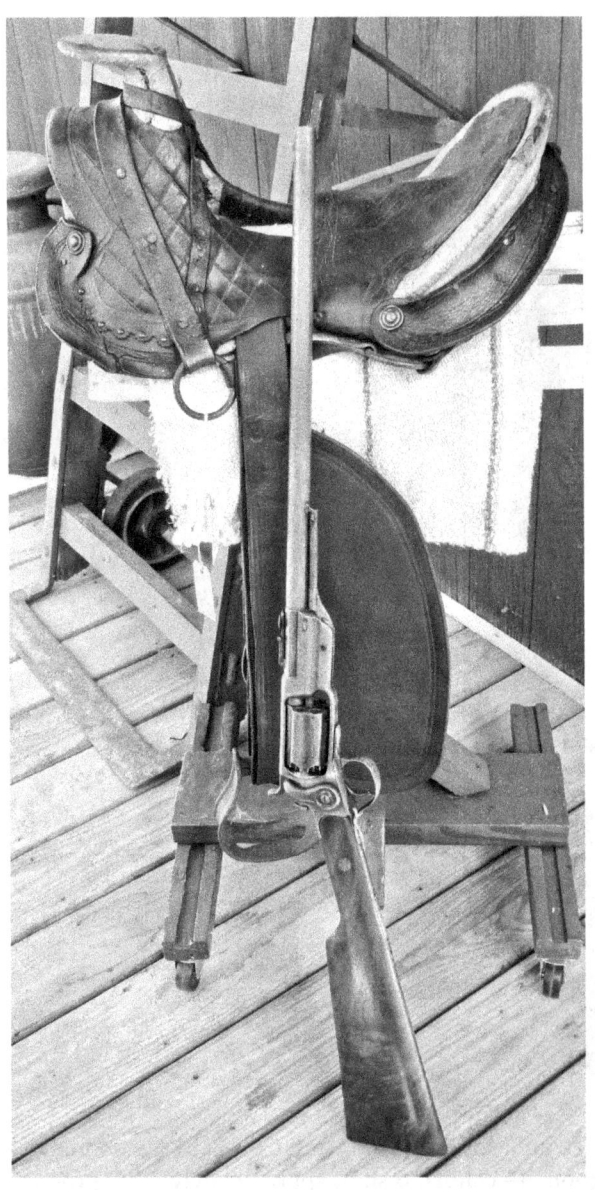

4-4 Colt Model 1855 revolving carbine: One of the very first multiple shot carbines, the model 1855 was popular with Texas Rangers. This example is a .36 caliber, 6 shot and mfg in circa 1858. Colt produced a total of 4,435 between 1856 and 1864. Also pictured is a Hope saddle circa 1850's. (Author's collection)

4-5 Colt Second Model Dragoon and Colt Baby Dragoon: Second model U.S. Dragoon .44 caliber, 6 shot, approximately 2700 produced. Second model is the scarcest of the Dragoon models. This example was mfg in early 1850. Baby Dragoon was a scaled down version of the larger Dragoons. It is a 5 shot, .31 caliber revolver. This one has a rolled cylinder scene of Texas Rangers fighting Comanche Indians. It was mfg in 1849. (Author's collection)

CHAPTER 5

THE CIVIL WAR

At the conclusion of the Mexican War of 1946-48, the Rangers returned home but not to a state of tranquility. There was always the treat of hostile Indians and Mexican bandits. During the ten years of Texas as a sovereign Republic much of the recourses were devoted to a two front war; Indians to the north and Mexicans to the south. Now that it was part of the United States, the federal government was responsible for defense against the Indians. In the absence of federal military protection, Governor George T. Wood ordered six Ranger Companies mustered for the immediate Indian crisis. One Ranger Captain who achieved notoriety was John Salmon Ford or "Old Rip." As early in the mid 1850's the State of Texas provided weapons to the Rangers. When equipment was lost, company commanders filed claims against the state. The handgun of choice appears to have been Colts. 44 caliber Dragoon Model Revolver along with a double barrel shotgun. Both suited for close in fighting. Subsequent requisitions from the executive department of Texas to the U.S. Bureau of Ordnance indicated a preference to the Colts repeating rifle. The rifle had a revolving cylinder similar to the Colts pistol and was deemed the rifle particularly adapted to border warfare. Derived from the Walker model Colt, the Dragoon pistol was a better built more streamlined and more efficient weapon. It was the same caliber as the Walker and at 4 lb 2 oz was lighter. It was produced with slight variations from 1848 to 1862.

The Colts Dragoon was the first revolver formally adopted by the regular U.S. Army. By the late 1850's virtually every U.S. regiment of Mounted Rifles carried these revolvers. These revolvers served federal troops as well as state Rangers during all the hostile Indian incursions during the 1850-1861 time frames.

On February 1, 1861 the state convention adopted a resolution for submission declaring Texas a sovereign state. It went public on 20 February. Also in February, secessionists captured San Antonio. One by one military posts in Texas surrendered. Some federal military units destroyed weapons so they did not fall into the hands of state forces. Sam Houston was removed from office for refusing to take an oath of allegiance to the Confederacy. As Texas prepared for defensive action, famous Rangers like Rip Ford, Saul Ross and Ben McCullogh who started the war commanding Ranger units, were now transferring to the Confederacy. The 8th Texas Cavalry known as Terry's Texas Rangers was named after their deceased Commander Col. B. F. Terry who was killed in the Battle of Woodsonville, Kentucky in December 1861. Numerous civil war battles were fought not only in the eastern states but also in Texas.

During the civil war era, 1861–1865 the United States saw a massive explosion in firearms technology and design. When the rebellion started most soldiers and Rangers were using single shot rifles. The lucky few had a multi shot Colt revolver or Colts Model 1855 revolving rifle. By the close of the war in 1865, the lever action Henry rile in .44 caliber rim fire revolutionized the rapid fire multi shot capabilities and greatly increased the killing ability of its user. With its 24 inch barrel it could hold 15 shots without reloading. This rifle was the forefather of the line of Winchester lever action carbines and rifles. New technological developments in 1863 and 1864 allowed Union carbines to be loaded and fired multiple times from an open breech. Names such as Smith, Burnside, Spencer, Joslynn, Starr and Maynard produced very fine carbines. Cavalry models had the saddle ring attachment on the left side where a shoulder sling snap hook could be attached. For security this prevented its being accidentally dropped from horseback. Most popular among the Civil War era carbines was the Sharps New Model 1859, 1863 and 1865 carbines. This early .52 caliber breech loader was so called "the straight breech model." Over 115,000 Sharps rifles were made from 1859 to 1866. Many of these reliable rifles were carried back to Texas from the Eastern battlefields. So popular was the Sharps carbine that after the close of the rebellion the State of Texas purchased many for issue to the Texas Rangers. We will discuss that later in the next chapter.

As Texas and the Confederacy prepared for war the lines between a purely state ranger force and the Army of a national government became blurred. This produced a confusing period in Ranger history. The genuine Ranger was still a citizen volunteer called into service to defend the frontier of the state. Early in the year 1862 Indian raids were light, due in part to a smallpox epidemic that broke out among the Plains tribes. By the end of the year, raiding had resumed. Both Union and Confederate agents kept the Indians stirred up, hoping the Indian raiding on the frontier would hurt the war effort of the other. The famous Texas cattleman, Oliver Loving reported that he saw a large number of Comanche with four to five thousand horses claimed to be stolen from Texas. These Indians were fed by U.S. forts on the Arkansas and paid by US troops for all scalps taken from Texans. The allegation that US troops were buying hair is most likely exaggerations. It is true however, that they were encouraging raids. There were many Indian raids along the frontier during the Civil War. They never seemed to stop. Even in the interwar years the U.S. army and Texas Rangers were not able to completely halt these hostile Indian forays. The limited numbers of Confederate troops in Texas were mainly concerned with military matters. The Texas Rangers and civilian authorities were sometimes overwhelmed. It is estimated that from 1862 to the last major Indian fight of the Civil War time period, over 400 Texans were killed, wounded or carried off into captivity by Indians. The last major Indian fight in the Civil War period was fought at Dove Creek near what is now San Angelo in January 1865.

The massive amount of small arms produced during the civil war years 1861-1865 totaled numbers never imagined. Now there was no shortage of available firearms to the Texas frontier citizens. It was now possible for every settler to purchase at least one dependable pistol and rifle. With all the available firepower, the days of the hostile Southern Indians were coming to a close

CHAPTER 5

ILLUSTRATIONS

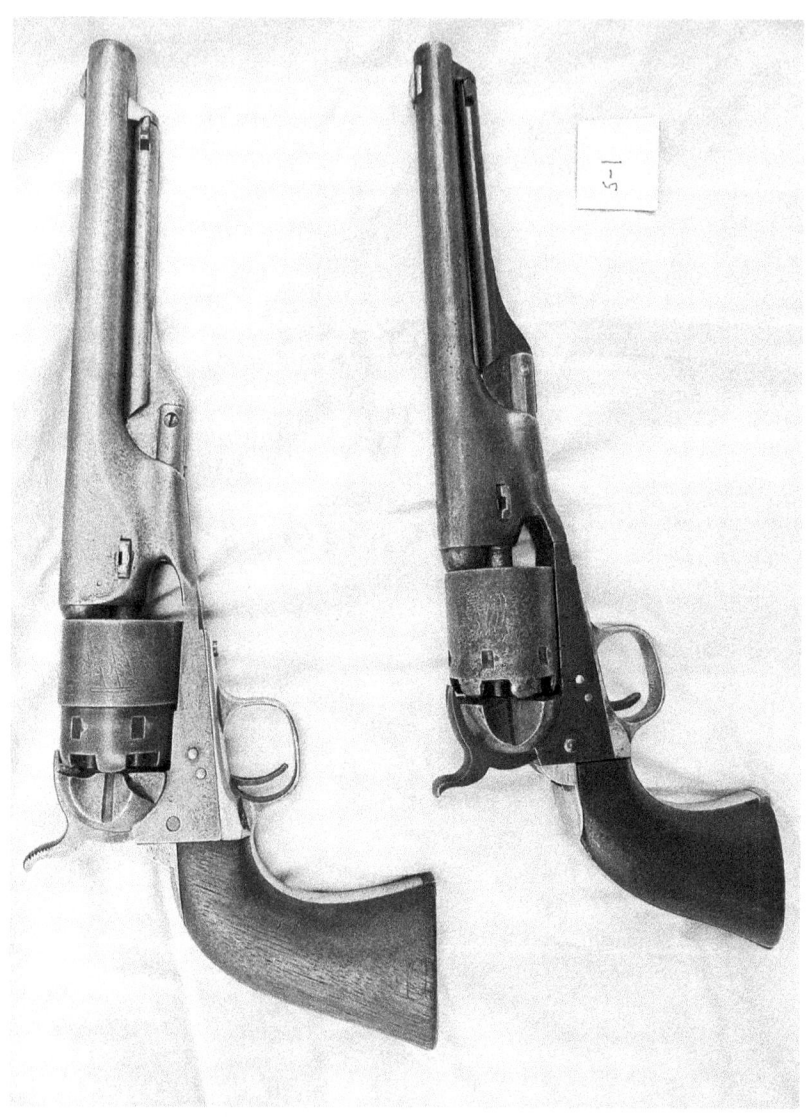

5-1 Colt model 1860 Army and 1861 Navy: *Left*–1860 single action army was the most popular Colt of the period. .44 caliber, 6 shot percussion, this example mfg 1862. *Right*–1861 Colt Navy .36 caliber, 6 shot, an improved version of the 1851 Navy. This example mfg 1863. (Author's collection)

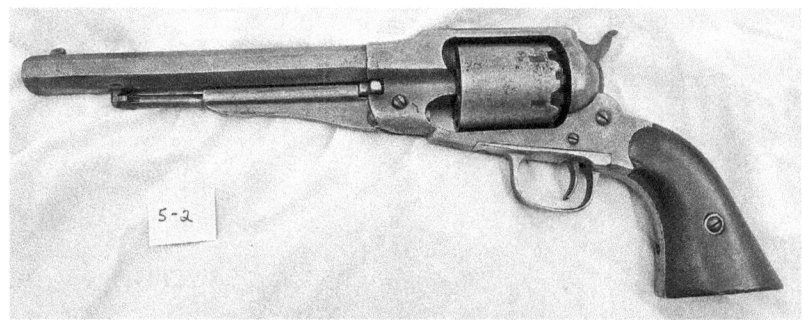

5-2 Remington New Model Army: Second most popular Civil War Union revolver .44 caliber, 6 shot, single action percussion revolver. Example mfg circa 1864. (Author's collection)

5-3 Starr Army revolvers 3rd most marketed Union Revolver: *Top*–Model 1858 Army, double action, .44 caliber percussion, 6 shot with 6 inch round barrel. Example mfg 1860. *Bottom*–single action Army .44 caliber, percussion, 6 shot with 8 inch barrel. Example mfg 1864. (Author's collection)

5-4 C. Sharps rifle and carbine: *Left*–1863 New Model military musket, .52 caliber percussion. Example mfg 1864. *Right*–Saddle ring cavalry carbine. New model 1864, 50/70 centerfire caliber. Example mfg 1864. (Author's collection)

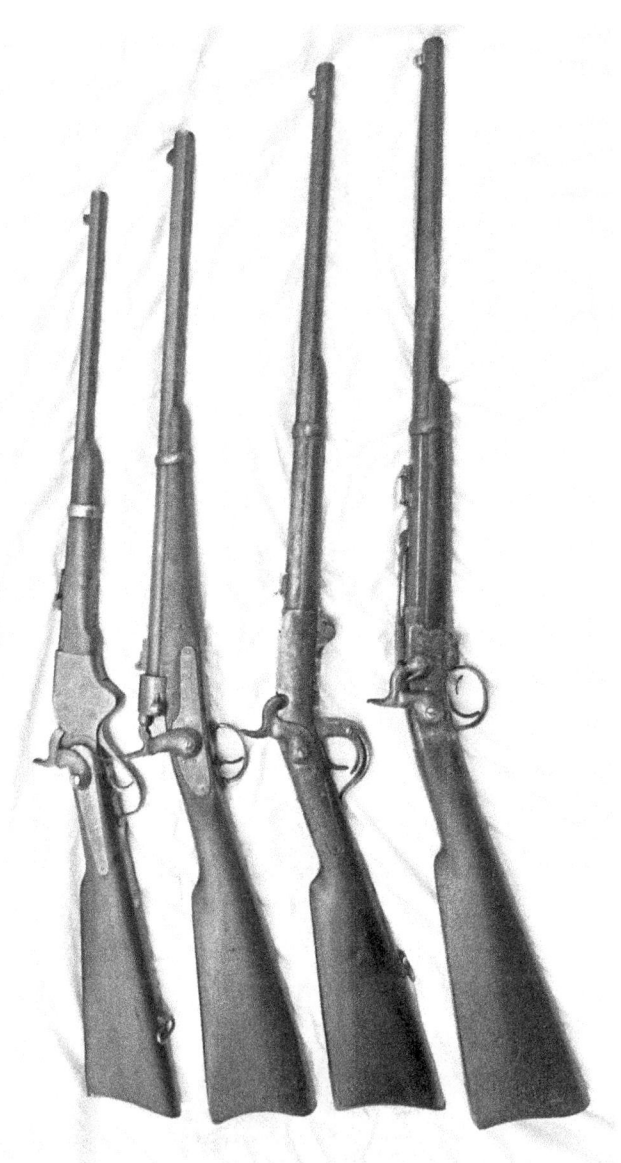

5-5 Grouping of Civil War carbines: *Left* to *right*–Spencer carbine, .52 caliber rimfire. This example mfg 1865; Joselyn Firearms Co. .52 caliber, mfg 1864; Burnside Rifle Company 4th model .54 caliber, mfg circa 1863; Smith Carbine, .50 caliber, Massachusetts Arms Company mfg circa 1863. (Author's collection)

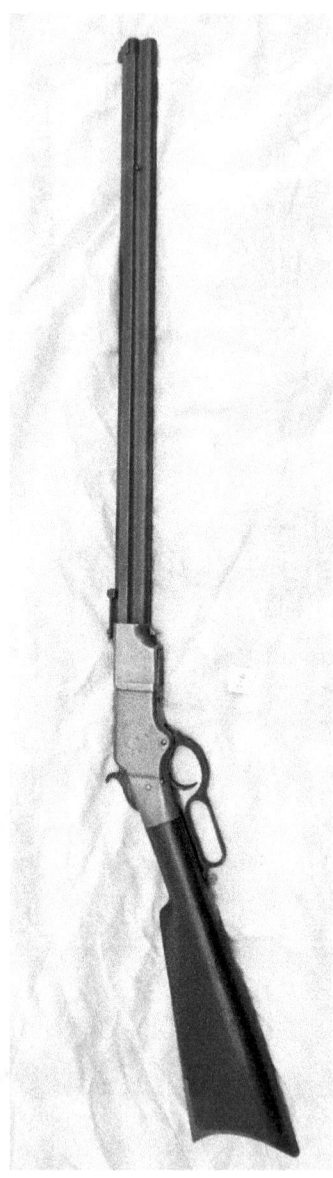

5-6 Henry model 1860 lever action rifle, .44 caliber rimfire. This late version was known as a "round top" and manufactured in 1866. This example is one of the last 10 documented Henry's manufactured. The Henry was the grandfather of all the line of Winchester lever actions that followed. (Author's collection)

CHAPTER 6

THE TIME OF RECONSTRUCTION

When the War Between the States or Civil War officially ended in 1865, many war weary Confederate soldiers returned to Texas. Sometimes the only thing of value was the pistol or rifle taken from Northern troops on some distant battlefield. One of the only things plentiful at this time was military firearms. Tired, poor, hungry and well armed, these ex-soldiers returned to a Texas devastated by over 4 years at war. It has been said that to the victor go the spoils. This seemed to be true in post war Texas. The only major group of people with money was the Northern supporters and those eager to come into Texas from Eastern states. These speculators and money grubbers became known as "carpet baggers." Maybe because they came to ravished Texas with a carpetbag full of Yankee money. The Confederate currency was worthless long before the close of the hostilities. When the Texas government during reconstruction levied taxes on cash poor settlers, they often lost their homes and properties. The state police organized during this time was highly despised and had a reputation of being corrupt. It lasted only 3 years and the fact that over 1/3 of its personnel were freedmen did little to enhance its image.

Well what happened to the Rangers? They came back with the passage of the 1870 Frontier Defense Act. It authorized the muster of 20 companies of Texas Rangers for 12 month service. As usual Rangers were to provide horses, six shooters and accoutrements. For the first time, however, the shoulder arm breech loading cavalry carbines would be purchased by the state. These were of the Sharps saddle ring carbine. The state was also to provide ammunition and forage. By the end of 1870 a total of 14 companies had been organized and posted at key locations on the frontier. These Davis Rangers preformed well from autumn 1870 until June 1871 when the last company was mustered out. It would be until 1874 before the Texas Rangers became formally institutionalized. As mentioned, these Rangers were required to provide their own six-guns. What exactly were they carrying: most common would be pistols brought home from the Civil War battlefields. Models such as the Colt 1851 Navy in .36 caliber, 1860 Army model Colt in .44 caliber. The reference to Army or Navy at this time period did not refer to its actual usage. It was the practice to refer to pistols of .36 caliber as Navy Models and those of the .44 caliber as Army models. The Colt Model 1860 Army saw widespread use during the period of reconstruction. In production from 1860 to 1873, a total of about 200,500 were made. It was the major revolver in use by US Troops in the Civil War. It had an eight inch barrel and a cylinder with a rolled scene of a naval engagement. The 1860 Army with its larger more powerful .44 caliber and its increased stopping power made it a highly effective weapon. Also well represented was the Remington Army revolver in .44 caliber. It was the second most issued Union revolver and was followed in quantity by the Starr Model .44 revolver. Starr produced 2 models one in single and one in double action. Some of the early frontier pistols made in Confederate factories such as the .36 caliber navy model brass frame Griswald and Gunnison revolver were carried in limited quantities.

Also carried in limited quantities was the LaMat designed by Dr. Jean Alexander LeMat of New Orleans. This weapon was different in that it was a two barrel revolver with main barrel 9 shot .42 caliber with a center barrel of .63 caliber that could also be selected. But then again, this was Texas and Rangers just liked their Colts. In the year 1871, smith and Wesson released their large frame .44 S&W caliber break open revolver. Known as the First Model American, it was the first factory .44 revolvers to legally fire a metallic self contained cartridge. Early in 1871 the U.S. Army purchased a total of 1,000 of these revolvers for their Federal Cavalry units.

One note of interest about the Texas Rangers between the 1870 and 1900s, they did not carry or wear badges. If they did have a badge it was obtained individually and was commonly made from the large size silver peso also known as an 8 reales coin. One early badge is pictured in this chapter dated 1894 made from an 8 reales. After 1900 Rangers were pictured to wear badges but not all.

Now back to the year 1874. This was the year credited for founding the frontier battalion. It was probably the best organized and best disciplined Ranger unit of the nineteenth century. It was commanded by 39 year old Major John B. Jones. He was a no nonsense, get the job done type of leader. The Captains who served under him were dedicated Rangers however they had their hands full. The decade of the 1870's was to be known as the Terrible Seventies. This period of turmoil is discussed in more detail in Chapter 7 known as the Time of the Outlaws. The Mason County war and numerous feuds such as the DeWitt County's' notorious Taylor/Sutton feud, led to the formation of a special unit. This unit was known informally as the Special Force of Texas State Troops or McNellys Rangers named after is commanding officer Captain Leander H. McNelly. They answered to Attorney General Steele and they were professional, full time lawmen. My relative John B. Armstrong served as a Sergeant under Captain McNelly. As a lieutenant he is known for his role in capturing the outlaw John Wesley Hardin at Pensacola, Florida in 1877. He was also there when Sam Bass died in Round Rock and was instrumental in the capture of John King Fisher. Lieutenant John B. Armstrong was a true Texas Ranger hero. I will discuss the exploits of the Special Force in another chapter. Now that the Civil War was over, Texas found itself an occupied province subject to the priorities of is Northern conquerors. These priorities were much different from those on the frontier.

CHAPTER 6

ILLUSTRATIONS

6-1 Colt 1860 Army Conversion and Colt 1851 Navy Conversion: *Top–* 1860 Army model, Richards Conversion to .44 centerfire, self contained cartridge. One piece carved ivory grips with Mexican eagle and snake, converted circa 1877. *Bottom–* 1851 Navy converted to .38 centerfire cartridge, 5 inch octagon barrel with 2 piece vintage ivory grips, mfg circa 1875 (Author's collection)

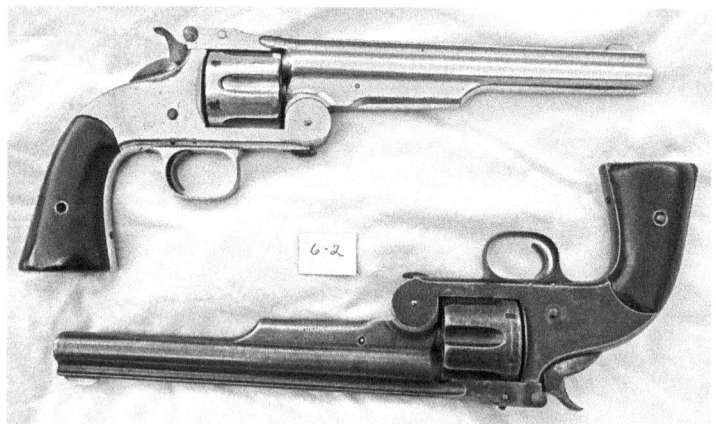

6-2 Smith and Wesson First Model American: First self contained metallic cartridge revolver purchased by the United States government. 1000 purchase for cavalry units on the frontier .44 S & W caliber, 6 shot, 8 inch barrel, single action. One example nickel plated and one blue finish U.S. contract revolvers. Both manufactured in 1871. (Author's collection)

6-3 Eli Whitney pocket revolver and Allen Wheelock side hammer revolver: *Top*–6 shot .31 caliber percussion revolver made by the Eli Whitney Company in New Haven, Ct. mfg 1860. *Bottom*–Allen and Wheelock 3rd model in .32 caliber rim fire, made by Allen and Wheelock, Worchester, MS mfg 1861. (Author's collection)

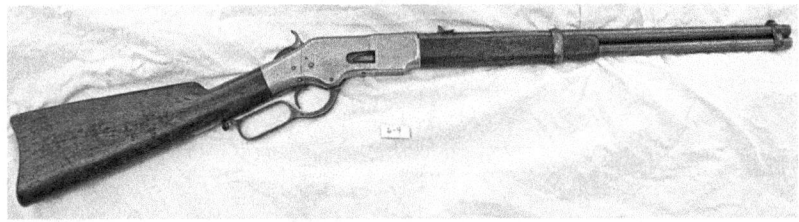

6-4 Winchester Model 1866 carbine: Known as the "Yellow Boy" .44 caliber rim fire, the same cartridge fired in the Henry rifle- brass frame, lever action, saddle ring carbine. Example is a 4th model mfg in 1876. (Author's collection)

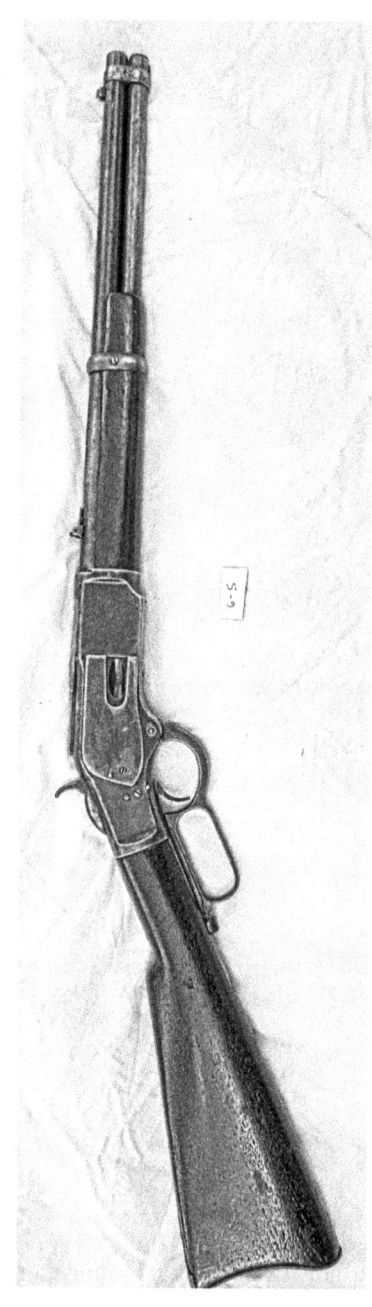

6-5 Winchester Model 1873 carbine Lever action saddle ring carbine .44 caliber center fire, short barrel version known as a "trapper" model. Example is a second model mfg in 1879. (Author's collection)

CHAPTER 7

TIME OF THE OUTLAWS

As we mentioned in Chapter 6, the period of the 1870's was referred to as the Terrible 70's. I would go further and call it, the time of the outlaw. Not only was there a continuing danger from hostile Indians and Mexican incursion from the south and west, but now it was the time of the Texas outlaw. Criminals such as Sam Bass, John Wesley Hardin, John King Fisher, Ben Thompson and Bill Longley were some of the most notable outlaws of the period. It was also the time of the self contained metallic cartridge revolvers. Rapid reloading was now common place.

In 1873 Colt came out with their single action Army revolver in .45 caliber long colt. It was Colt's first original factory produced .45 caliber revolver firing the self contained metal centerfire cartridge. Prior to 1873, Colt produced a modified .44 caliber revolver (1871-1872). It was a factory adaption of the Model 1860 Army model which was a percussion firearm. It was called an open top because it did not have a solid top strap like the later Model 1873 SSA. A previous market model was merely a modified 1860 Army revolver converted to fire a .44 caliber metallic rimfire cartridge and was called a conversion model for obvious reasons. You might be asking why Colt waited until 1873 to come out with a pure factory produced revolver with a metallic cartridge that loaded from the rear of the cylinder. The answer is that Smith and Wesson made a very profitable purchase when they obtained the patent held by Rollin White. Colt tried numerous times to purchase the patent with no results. Holding this patent allowed Smith and Wesson in 1871 to come out with a break open large frame revolver under the same above specifications. It was called the First Model American and fired a .44 Smith and Wesson self contained metallic cartridge. It wasn't until 1873 when the Rollin White patent expired, that Colt could le-gally produce the revolver we now know as the Peacemaker or Single Action Army revolver model 1873. This Colt .45 became to identify the image of the Texas Rangers for decades to come. Who could picture an old west Ranger or outlaw without the trusty Peacemaker strapped to their hips? Colt, who from the onset out marketed Smith and Wes-son, had a vast advantage on the western markets. Smith and Wesson concentrated on marketing their .44 caliber revolvers mainly to foreign markets with large contracts going to the Russian government. This left Colt a free hand to dominate the western markets.

Some foreign fire arms manufacturers achieved limited western sales. One such company was the English firm, Adams Patent Small Arms Company. Some of the English Webley R.I.C. #1 and #2 revolvers in .45 caliber were also seen in limited numbers. Ever since the sale of the Paterson Colt, the first Colt marketed in Texas, Texans have favored their revolvers over all others. The Peacemaker became the main stay of the Ranger force. A six shot single action Army revolver was originally marketed only in .45 caliber long Colt and with a 7 1/2 inch barrel. It was later produced in 36 different calibers with many special order combinations available. The most popular caliber was .45 long Colt (150,683 made) and 44/40 (64,439 made). Other popular calibers were .41, 38/40 and 32/20 Colt. History shows that the vast majority of early Texas Rangers chose the 45 SAA as their service weapon of choice. My relative and famous Texas Ranger, Lieutenant John Barkley Armstrong is known to have used his 7 ½ inch barrel Colt .45 to sub-due and capture John Wesley Hardin. This all transpired in a railroad car at Pensacola, Florida in 1877. When Hardin saw the Colt .45 he is reported to have said "Texas, by God." Hardin was not fast enough and it all ended when the 7 ½ inch barrel of Lt Armstrong's Colt SAA came crashing down on John Wesley's scull. At the time of his capture, John Wesley Hardin was the most wanted man in the nation. He is said to have killed over 40 men; one for merely snoring. After many years of imprisonment at Huntsville, Texas he was released in 1893 only to be shot in El Paso, Texas by Constable John Selman in 1895. Constable

Selman used a .45 Colt single action Army revolver and shot Hardin from behind. Hardin was carrying two Colt Model 1877 double action revolvers at the time of his death. These .41 DA caliber revolvers were known as Thunderer Models and two were found on his body. He was also known on occasion to have carried a Smith and Wesson flip open pocket revolver.

Almost as notorious was the outlaw, train robber, Sam Bass. After numerous robberies out of state and around north Texas, Sam Bass and his gang attempted to rob the bank in Round Rock Texas. His failed endeavor resulted in his death on July 21, 1878 from gunshot wounds received during the attempt. Bass was said to have been carrying a 7 ½ inch barrel Colt single action in 44/40 caliber. This caliber was known as "Frontier Six" and was only marketed one year earlier in 1877. Less notable was the outlaw John King Fisher. He was captured by Ranger Lieutenant Lee Hall in May 1877. Hall was made First Lieutenant on 22 January, 1877 when the Special Force was reorganized. John B. Armstrong was made 2nd Lieutenant and McNelly's name was no longer used to identify the Force. On May 16, Lt Hall wired Austin that he had "Arrested King Fisher and others charged along with Ben Thomson with the killing of Wilson in Austin." Mark Wilson was a gambler murdered in Austin, Texas. The deaths of Fisher, Thompson and John Wesley Hardin accounted for three of the "big four' bad men. In spite of dozens of killings of their combined records only Bill Longley paid the extreme penalty. He died on the gallows in Giddings, east of Austin on October 11, 1878.

There is an interesting story about Lt. John B. Armstrong as told to me by my late mother, whose maiden name was Armstrong, and served as the curator of the Layland Museum in Cleburne, Texas. The story goes that my great grandfather John D. Armstrong went to a cattle sale near Austin in the 1880's where he ran into John Barkley Armstrong who was then a retired Ranger and cattle rancher. As they began talking they quickly discovered that they were both Armstrong's and became instant friends. John B traded my great grandfather a Colt .45 SAA for a Winchester rifle. The pistol that I donated to the Texas Ranger Museum in Waco is said to be this Colt. It is located in the first display case on the left as you walk into the museum. It has a placard that states "pistol owned by John B. Armstrong and donated by the family of Robert D. Moser." All the principals in the story are deceased, but as the old saying goes "Go with the legend"

Our image of the outlaw or the Ranger wearing his Colt is paramount in the minds of most. Remington also produced two models, the 1875 and 1890 frontier style 6 shooters in 44/40 Winchester centerfire caliber. Remington marketed these revolvers to compete with the Colt Peace Maker but neither was well received. Production totals of the Model 1890 revolver totaled approximately 5,000. Another firearms manufacturer not mentioned before and one that was represented on the frontier was the Merwin and Herbert. The Merwin Herbert and Company, New York City marketed this 6 shot, 7 inch barrel frontier revolver in .44 M&H and .44 Russian calibers centerfire. These revolvers were actually manufactured by the company of Hopkins and Allen, Norwich, Connecticut, USA. It has a unique extraction and loading mechanism. The barrel with top strap twisted sideways and when pulled forward with the cylinder attached, extracts the cartridges. These revolvers were made 1876 to 1880. Movie buffs might recall the western "The Long Riders" about the James Younger gang. In the movie, it has one of the gang carrying a Merwin Herbert .44 revolver. Another name that appears in the old west is the firm of Parker Brothers. They produced a line of fine double barrel shotguns. Many with shortened barrels were used to guard freight wagons and stage coaches. Known as "sawed off shotguns" they carried easily and had a broader scatter pattern. The "sawed off shotgun" in 10 and 12 gauges were the badest of the bad and the most feared weapon in the 1870's. You could say they were real attention getters. Just as a closing note there is an interesting story from the famous Texas Ranger James B. Gillett. He served 1877 to 1881. He relates that as a youth he purchased an old confederate musket for $3.50. This smooth bore musket although useful in hunting birds and squirrels led to the revelation that the kick from its recoil was so great that "it would get meat at both ends."

CHAPTER 7

ILLUSTRATIONS

7-1 Colt open top Model 1871: This was an interim model and bridged the gap between the 1860 self contained rimfire cartridge conversion model and the Model 1873. This early nickel plated model has one piece ivory grips with the Mexican national eagle and snake carved on it. It was manufactured in 1871. (Author's collection)

7-2 Adams revolver: Imported from England, the Adams was a well made dependable revolver used throughout the world. It saw limited use on the Texas frontier. Example is in .450 British caliber and was manufactured in 1872. (Author's collection)

7-3 Merwin Herbert and Co. single action revolver: Frontier six shooter with 7 inch barrel firing 6 shots of .44 Russian centerfire or .44 M&H caliber. Pictured is an early open top square butt frontier revolver in .44 Russian caliber; manufactured in 1878. (Author's collection)

7-4 Colt single action Army: Probably the most recognized hand gun in the world. A dependable strong top strap revolver originally available in .45 long colt caliber. Example is a 7 ½ inch barrel long colt manufactured in 1874 and later engraved to commemorate service of Texas Ranger Lt. John B. Armstrong. (Author's collection)

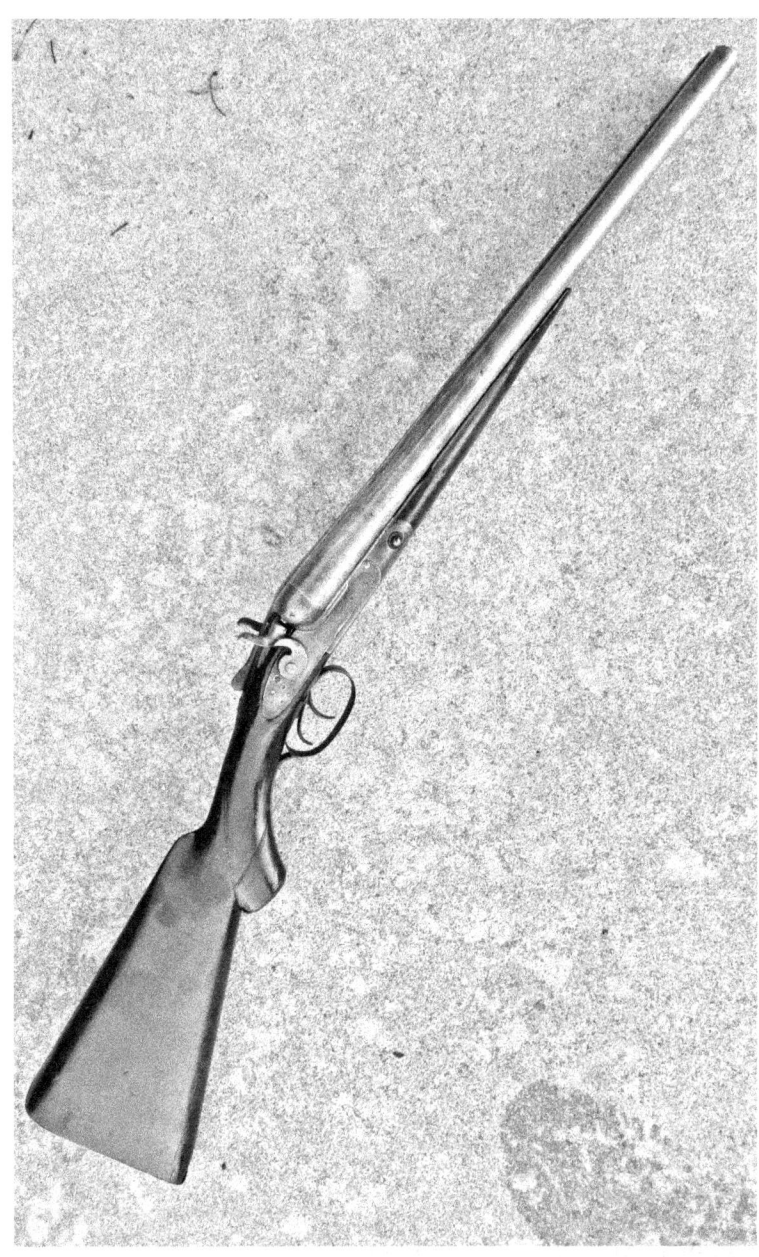

7-5 Double barrel shotgun (carriage gun): Example of an early stagecoach or carriage gun made by the Parker Brothers in 1882. It is a 12 gauge, top leaver shotgun with 18.5 inch Damascus barrels. (Author's collection)

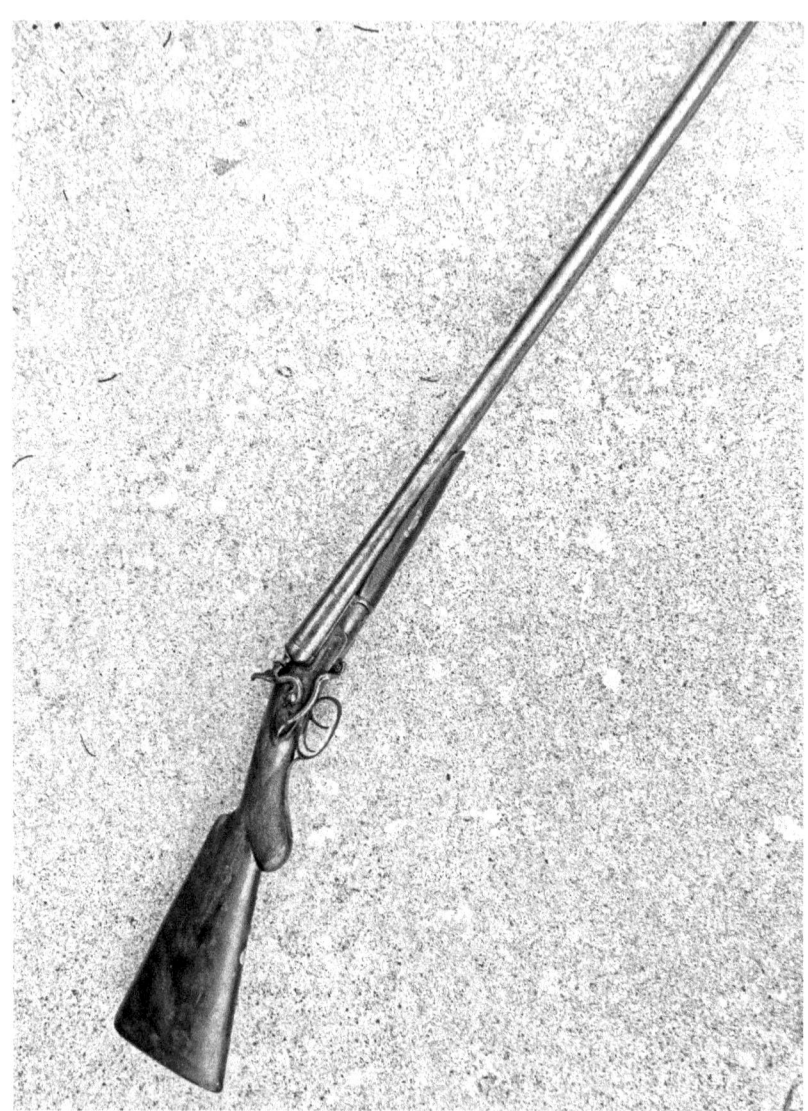

7-6 Double barrel shotgun: Early Wesley Richards 10 gauge side lever double barrel shotgun with 32 inch fine twist Damascus barrels was mfg in 1869. This fine English import is typical of the better made shotguns of the 1860's. (Author's collection)

CHAPTER 8

MARCHING TOWARD THE CENTURY

The last Indian fight in Texas occurred on January 29, 1881. Texas Ranger Captain Baylor caught up with a raiding band of Apaches in their camp in the Diablo Mountains west of Guadalupe Peak. Eight Indians were killed including women and children and several others were captured. Covered by blankets the Rangers couldn't distinguish warriors from the others. Captain Baylor was never pleased with the outcome of this battle. The days of the traditional Texas Ranger were over. Major Jones died also in 1881 and prompted the resignation of many leading Frontier Battalion Captains. Although the Battalion lingered on until 1900, there was really no need for it. The frontier line as we knew it no longer existed. Texas had no more Indians to fight and the few gun fighters and bad men that remained were starting to feel their age. More and more of the state law enforcement needs were being met by the local sheriffs and police. The Texas frontier by the mid 1890's was reduced to an isolated strip starting at Brownsville and running north following the river to El Paso. The city of El Paso had become the biggest thing in the Trans–Pecos. The arrival of railroads in 1881 boosted the city until it had 13,000 residents in 1895. Down river, peace was being established under the watchful eye of the Texas Rangers and Judge Roy Bean. Despite Judge Roy Bean's ruthlessness he never hanged anyone. He was for good or bad; the only law in the Pecos region and the Rangers were more than willing to back him.

The Texas Rangers still favored their Colt Peacemakers in .45 long colt caliber. After 1877 it was available in 44/40 caliber. This made carrying ammunition simpler as Winchester was marketing their model 1866 and 1873 carbines in the same 44/40 cartridge. Now a Ranger could use the same bullet in his pistol and his rifle. This also became convenient for the 38/40 chambered Colts and Winchester when it was marketed in 1886. This smaller caliber did not have wide appeal to the Rangers who preferred their 45's but found popularity amount cowboys and average citizens. The ever popular Winchester model 1873 lever action rifles and carbines were the most utilized long arm on the frontier.

The state of Texas provided the Model 1873 rifle for $50.00 each and $40.00 for the carbine. Although these weapons were provided by the state, the cost again fell to the individual Ranger. This debt was repaid by monthly deductions in his pay. Back in 1875 ten Rangers from Captain Roberts' Company D were willing to pay the cost for this superior arm. The lever action Winchester Model 1873 saw the widest period of usage of all four models of lever action Winchesters. Its dependability was testified by Texas Ranger George Lloyd. Lloyd was one of Lieutenant Jays' Company A Rangers. In 1879 along with 5 other Rangers, he was involved in an Indian fight during a scout in Las Cornudas with 12 hostiles. During the intense battle Lloyd accidentally loaded a .45 caliber cartridge in his 44/40 Winchester causing it to jam. Taking out his Bowie hunting knife, he calmly removed the screw and side plate on his model 73 Winchester and removed the jammed bullet. He replaced the side plate and continued the fight. It takes a man with iron nerve to do a thing like that. This brave determination seemed to be a quality shared by many frontier Rangers.

A larger model of the model 1873 Winchester was the model 1876 lever action rifle. It was Winchesters first major production of a large bore lever action. Usually chambered in larger more power cartridges such as the 45/60, 45/75 and 50/95, it looked to many like a model 1873 on steroids. They made over 63,000 of this model from 1876 to 1897.

Let us not forget the double action brother to the Colt 1873 Peacemaker. Less popular it still saw wide use in the west. Known as the Frontier Double Action Model 1878, it was very similar to the appearance of the Peacemaker. It is a 6 shot large frame revolver with standard calibers of 32/20, 38/40, .41 Colt, 44/40 and .45 Colt. One reason for it popularity was its chambering for the larger calibers and similarities to the single action army. Many well know figures on the frontier carried the Colt Model 1878. Numerous period photos of cowboys wearing what appears to be a peace maker, upon close examination is in reality a Model DA 1878 revolver. Colt also had limited success in marketing its smaller revolvers such as the New Line series in .38 and .41 calibers. The famous sharp shooter Annie Oakley is known to have carried a .41 caliber New Police Revolver. These down sized pistols were not much use in the Texas badlands but found limited popularity in larger cities. But then again the wild days for the frontier were fading fast.

Texas was racing to the turn of the 20th century and with it a new era for its state Rangers. This new century would bring new changes such as the Law of 1901 which did nothing but make Rangers peace officers, a legal technicality that simply legitimized what had been standard practice for 25 years. Under the Law of 1901, nothing changed, nothing was lost and nothing was gained. The four Captains, Hughes, Brooks, McDonald and Rodgers still commanded their four undersized companies. Texas still had its state police force. This segment of time leading to the 1900's would see a status quo in the Mexican border troubles. The Nueces Strip would remain a land in turmoil. Disputes along the Rio Grande between bandits and Rangers continued at the same exhausting pace. With the coming of the first decades of the 1900s a big change would come in the enforcement of law on the border.

CHAPTER 8

ILLUSTRATIONS

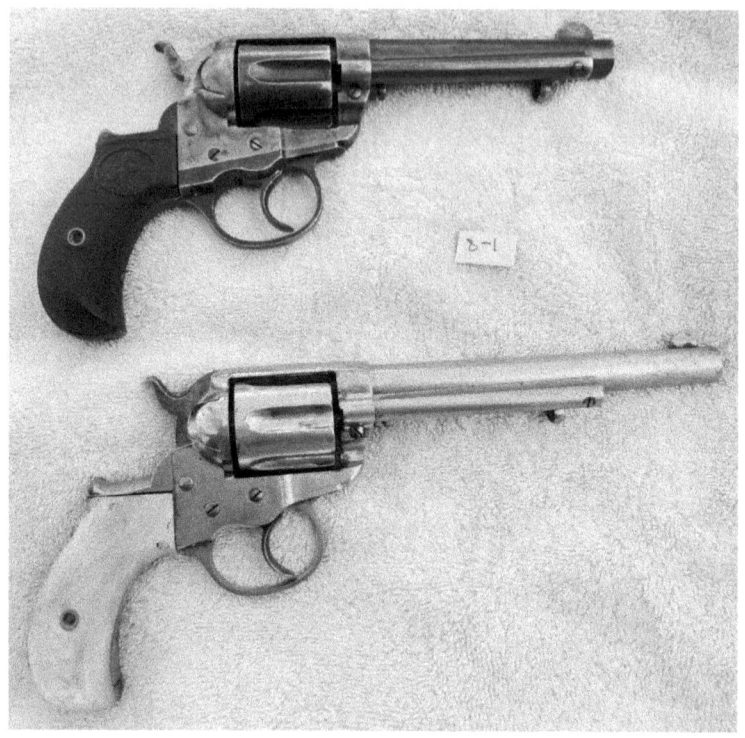

8-1 Colt DA Model 1877: Colts first double action revolver known as the 1877 Model. It came in .38 and .41 caliber versions. *Top*–revolver is the "Lightening" .38 caliber version mfg in 1901 Bottom–Factory nickel finish with mother of pearl grips .41 caliber "Thunderer" version mfg 1888. (Author's collection)

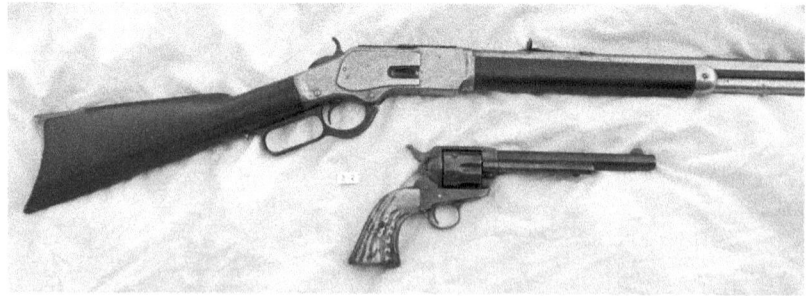

8-2 Winchester 1873 rifle and Colt SAA in 38/40: *Top*–Example of the Winchester 1873 octagon barrel rifle in 38/40 caliber mfg in 1884. *Bottom*–Colt SAA in 38/40 mfg 1902 both used the same Colt 38/40 cartridge. (Author's collection)

8-3 Winchester 1892 and Colt SAA in 44/40: *Top*–Winchester model 1892 saddle ring carbine in 44/40 mfg 1898. *Bottom*–Colt Single Action Army in 44/40 caliber mfg 1882. Both used the same 44/40 cartridge. (Author's collection)

8-4 Winchester Model 1876: First model for big bore lever action. The example is chambered in 45/75 center fire cartridge. It is a larger scale version of the Model 1873 rifle. Example mfg in 1882. (Author's collection)

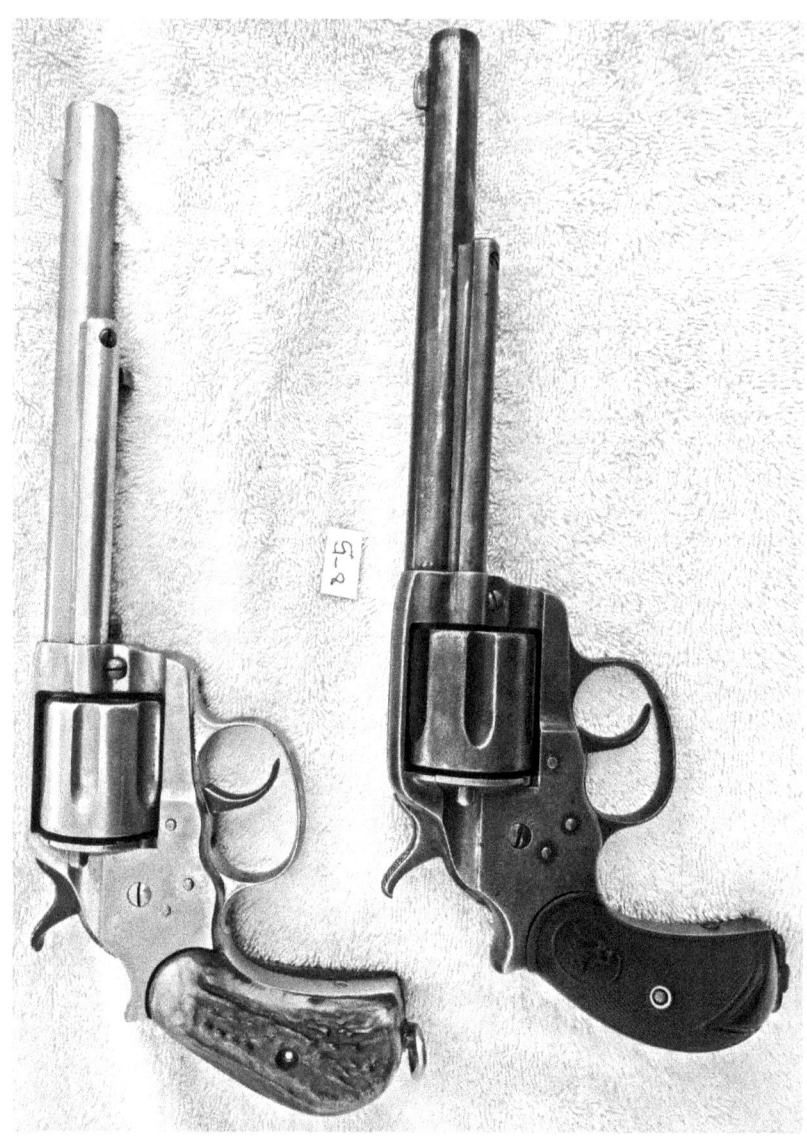

8-5 Colt DA model 1878: Double action large frame model saw wide use alongside its well known partner the Peacemaker. *Left*–Nickel finish 7 ½ barrel, 44/40 caliber mfg in 1883. *Right*–blue finish 7 ½ inch barrel .45 long Colt mfg 1899. (Author's collection)

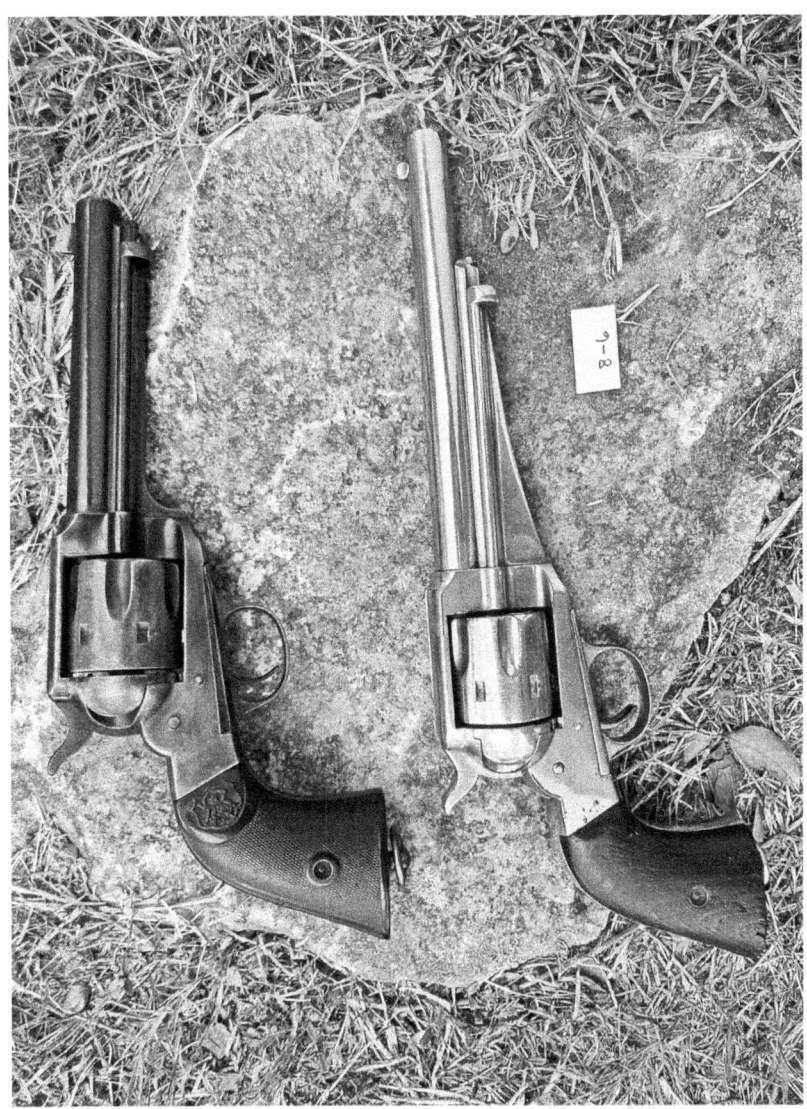

8-6 Remington Model 1875 and 1890 revolvers: *Left*–Model 1890 Remington single action revolver in 44/40 WCF. Mfg 1892. Remington tried to compete with sales of the Colt SAA. *Right*–Model 1875 Remington single action revolver in 44/40 WCF caliber. This example mfg 1877 is nickel plated platted and has provenance to Nez Perce Indian police. (Author's collection)

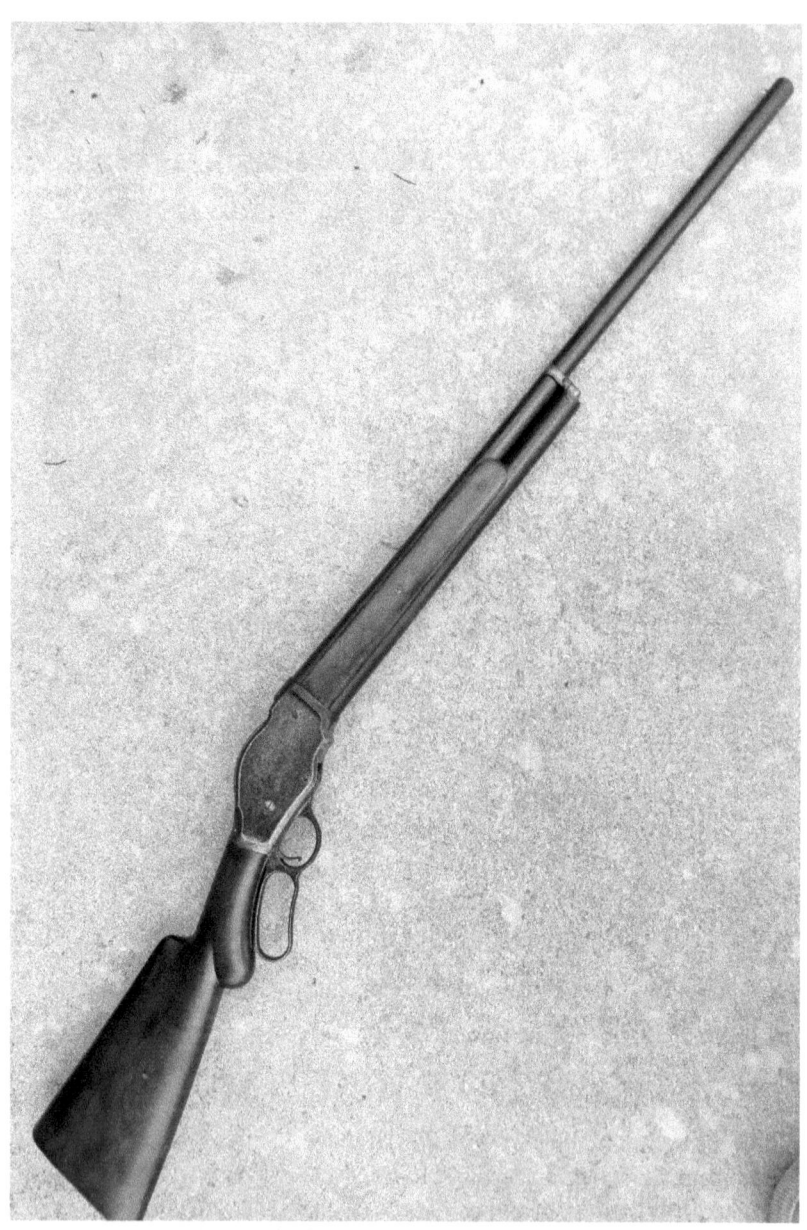

8-7 Winchester Model 1887 lever action shotgun: Winchester's first lever action 10 gauge shotgun. John Browning invented this rather massive scattergun. It achieved only moderate success. Example mfg 1890. (Author's collection)

CHAPTER 9

RANGERS AND THE CAVALRY

Since the time of the Mexican War, there has been a relationship between the U.S. Mounted Rifles (and later, U.S. Cavalry) and the Texas Rangers. During the time of the American Civil War, Terry's Texas Rangers were a Confederate cavalry unit. Texas after statehood had a long standing relationship between the state Rangers and the Federal Mounted Troops. The task of policing the hostile Indians on the frontier fell to the U.S. Army; at least that was the plan on paper. In reality the Texas Rangers took up the "slack." The frontier battalion was primarily concerned with cattle rustling and banditry along the southern border however, they were also involved with bringing a just due to raiding hostile Indian tribes.

The weapon of choice as we discussed earlier, was the Colt single action revolver in .45 long Colt caliber. This was also the issued service weapon for the United States Cavalry. From 1873 to 1891 the single action army revolver was the standard issue hand gun for the United States Cavalry units on the western frontier. Over 31,000 revolvers were purchased by the United States government over this 21 year period. The 10th and 8th Cavalry had a presence in Texas with the 10th Cavalry being stationed at Fort Davis in West Texas. The 10th Cavalry troopers were called buffalo soldiers by the native Indians. There have been numerous explanations for this name. As was the custom of the time only white officers could be in command. The Colt Cavalry model pistol was almost identical to the civilian model carried by Rangers and frontiersman. All U.S. model 1873 SAA's were in .45 long colt caliber, all had 7 ½ inch barrels and oiled walnut one piece pistol grips. Civilian versions after 1877 could be purchase in 44/40 caliber and later with 4 ¾ and 5 ½ inch barrels. The only obvious difference with the U.S. Model and the civilian counterpart was the presents of a stamped "U.S." on the left frame by the patent dates. The Cavalry Colts were worn on the right side in a butt forward flap holster. This regulation style influenced many frontiersmen. An example is Wild Bill Hickok who wore 2 Colt Navy's, butt forward, tucked into a waist belt. Many of the U.S. model Colts ended up in the hands of Native Americans as well as frontiersman and Texas Rangers, through many sources of procurement. The Texas Rangers acquired the 1st and 2nd U.S. Model Colt Dragoon revolvers in the 1850's from federal ordinance officers. A number of model 1873 Cavalry models were also provided to the State of Texas.

Another U.S. Cavalry weapon that saw widespread usage on the Texas frontier was the Springfield Model 1873 "trapdoor" saddle ring carbine. This short barrel carbine fired a large heavy bullet in 45/70 centerfire caliber. Texas Ranger Captain Baylor preferred his 45/70 rifle to his newly issued Winchester Model 1873 lever action rifle in 44/40 caliber. Captain Baylor who took over command of Company C, El Paso, Texas in 1879, employed a collapsible tripod set up that he called "rest sticks." This gave him increased accuracy through its stability. After all his Rangers went to the Winchester Model 1873's, he held stubbornly to his 45/70 sporting rifle. The 45/70 cartridge was first fielded with a copper casing. These were known to swell and jam in the rifle after repeated rapid fire use. This was a problem with the soldiers of the 7th Cavalry at the battle of the Little Big Horn. The military wisely converted to the brass cased shell soon afterwards. It is known that many frontier Rangers at one time or the other carried a Springfield "trapdoor" carbine. It would knock down a buffalo at relatively short ranges but due the weight of the bullet, it had an immediate drop in trajectory. This made it undesirable for long distance accuracy.

The relationship between the U.S. Army forces and the Texas Rangers was at times rocky. As the Army was conquering the Comanche's, Texas Rangers such as Captain Leander McNelly and his men were contending with Mexican stock thieves. Captain McNelly not only crossed the Rio Grande to violate Mexican sovereignty but also used intimidation and gun battles to carry out his cattle recoveries. On one raid in the 1870s he barely escaped annihilation from Mexican forces. His Ranger force was able to cross the Rio Grande leaving their horses behind due in part to the presence of U.S. Army troops guarding the American side. The U.S. troops had specific orders not to cross the Rio Grande. The presence of the U.S. Army troops persuaded the Mexican forces to withdraw.

The Texas Rangers and the U.S. Cavalry units shared a combined concern for the Mexican revolutionary Garza movement (1891 to 1893). These revolutionary patriots behaved like stereotypical Mexican bandits. In the first role they challenged the U.S. Cavalry to enforce neutrality laws. In the second role they challenged the Texas Rangers to enforce state laws. The Garza campaign earned neither the U.S. Cavalry nor the Texas Rangers any laurels. A few gunfights and a few captures scarcely offset the toil and frustration of constantly scouting an unforgiving land populated by unsympathetic Rancheros.

One of my fondest memories of the teamwork between Texas Rangers and the U.S. Cavalry is portrayed in the John Wayne movie "The Searchers." Although fictitious it shows a working relationship which actually existed between U.S. Cavalry units stationed in south Texas and the Rangers. In their fight between hostile Comanche Indians, they combined forces to attack a band led by a war chief called "Scar," in order to rescue white hostages. It is the kind of movie that helps promote a positive image of the Ranger force. It did not however, promote a positive image to those of Comanche decent. Even in our modern time there are many Comanche descendents who harbor very bitter feelings toward the Rangers.

As the Comanche's never formally surrendered there was a modern movement among the Texas Ranger supporters to enter into a signed peace agreement with the Comanche Nation. Retired Texas Ranger H. Joaquin Jackson met with leaders of the current Comanche Nation and presented this purely ceremonially request. After a short deliberation, the Comanche Nation denied the request. They could not forget the deprivations they felt were committed even after all these years. This feeling of non-forgiveness also exists with some of the Mexican Americans in south Texas. They still hold bitterness for harsh treatment from frontier Texas Rangers. As I stated in another chapter, Texas in the frontier era, was a harsh, dangerous unforgiving land. It took an individual such as the Texas Ranger to cope with its hardships and dangers. This many times was without any support other than that from a fellow Ranger. Violence was common across the land and it took violence and harsh methods to contain the situation. These methods were often misunderstood when examined during modern times. You would have to put yourself in the position of the early Ranger to fully appreciate the difficult job he had in enforcing law and order in a lawless wilderness.

CHAPTER 9

ILLUSTRATIONS

9-1 Example of Cavalry Trooper shell jacket as worn from Civil War until the late Indian War. Depicted with carbine sling pistol belt with holster. (Authors collection)

9-2 Examples of U.S. issued Colt Model 1873 single action Cavalry revolver. All were purchased in .45 long colt caliber, 7 ½ inch barrels with one piece walnut grips. *Left*–revolver was manufactured in 1874 and the *right*–manufactured in 1891. These are second and last year production examples. (Authors collection)

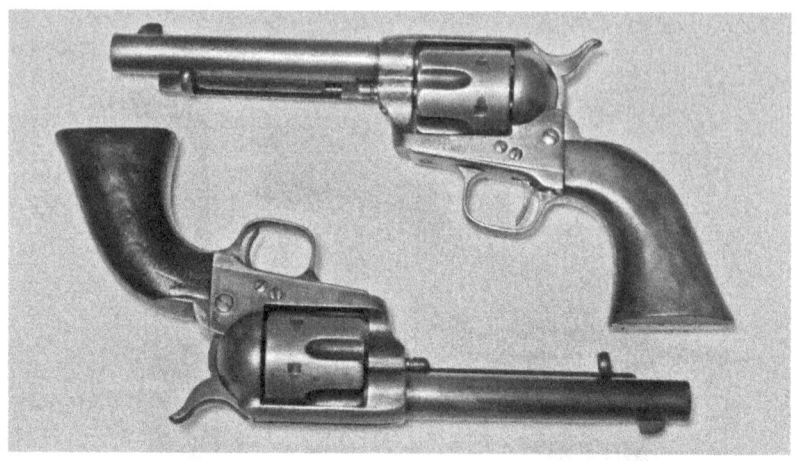

9-3 Examples of basic 7 ½ barrel cavalry Colts that were arsenal modified to 5 ½ inch barrels in the early 1900's and were referred to as Artillery Models. *Top*– example manufactured in 1878 and *bottom*–manufactured in 1883. (Authors collection)

9-4 U.S. Springfield Model 1873 45/70 "Trapdoor" saddle ring carbine. It was the standard issue carbine to all cavalry units on the Western frontier. Example manufactured 1880. (Authors collection)

CHAPTER 10

TURNING OF THE CENTURY

The 1900's started out with a big bang. Along the border the Rangers remained the men that Mexicans love to hate. Fuel to the fire was events such as the saga of Gregorio Cortez. Twenty six years old in 1901, he came from a family of horse thieves. Karnes County Sheriff, W. T. (Brack) Morris, a former Ranger attempted to arrest him on 21 June 1901. Cortez killed Sheriff Morris with three shots and hit the trail, dodging scores of pursuers. Cortez made a ten day run that spawned legends that would live forever on the Mexican border. In legend, Cortez turned from a horse thief into a simple tenant farmer. The Cerda brothers gained no such glory. The Cerda affair achieved prominence because political strife elevated it. Mexicans had been conditioned to believe the worst of Rangers and killing like that of the Cerda brothers easily translated into official executions. Rangers could usually justify their actions but never to Mexicans who had been reared on stories of Leander McNelly and Jack Hayes and who had seen their countrymen "bandits" or not gunned down by Rangers. Some revisionists even go as far as to claim that Rangers carried a rusty revolver in their saddle bags to drop beside a Mexican body when he claimed to kill in self defense.

Of all the tasks that the Rangers had to perform in the early 1900's none was more displeasing than enforcing prohibition. Rangers in Amarillo cleaned up the bowery operators and bootleggers but as soon as they left they reopened their businesses. Neither the sheriff nor local police intervened. This is just an example of how thankless and frustrating this work could be. After 1910 even as Ranger Captains

Rodgers and Hughes served out their remaining years, the Rangers sank into political mire. Some committed atrocities that would bring them again to the brink of distinction. Captain Hughes, however, did remain a pillar of morality. He retired in 1915 as Senior Captain after 28 years as a Ranger. In 1947 at age 92 and dying of cancer he took his own life.

Turn of the century Rangers still carried their trusted Colt Single Action Army revolvers in .45 long Colt. Lever action Winchester rifles and carbines 1892 and 1894 models were the long arms of choice for the Ranger force. The 1894 model has the longest production record and is still made currently. It was by far the most purchased of all the Winchesters. The only short comings of these carbines were in the relatively low velocity of the 44/40 and 30/30 cartridges. After 1900 a large number of Rangers favored the Winchester lever action model 1895. It was the last lever action model produced by Winchester. It has a fixed box magazine located beneath the frame. The most popular calibers were the 30/06 and the 30/40 krag smokeless high powered ammunition. Due to the box magazine the model 1895 has a distinctive profile, unlike any other Winchester rifle. There are numerous 1900 era pictures of Rangers holding their prized Model 1895 Winchesters. The Model 1895 was also popular with the Arizona State Rangers but was used more by Texans. One interesting story concerning the use of the Model 1895 by Texas Rangers happened in 1906. Ranger Captain McDonald, then stationed in Alice, Texas, was summoned to Starr County where an assassination attempt was made against District Judge Welch. In route Captain McDonald and his Rangers were ambushed near Rio Grand City at a point known as Casitas. Captain McDonald was carrying a new type semiautomatic weapon that jammed after the first shot. His Rangers using their reliable lever action Winchester Model 1895 saddle ring carbines saved the day. They left four Mexican bandits dead and two wounded. This event led many Rangers to distrust the new developments in semi-automatic weapons. Also in the year 1906 was when the famous Ranger Frank Hamer joined the force. He was accompanied by R. M. "Duke" Hudson. There is a famous photo of these two from 1906 taken in Alpine, Texas shortly after joining up. Duke Hudson served as a Texas

Ranger and later went on to be the two term Grimes County sheriff (circa 1924). He was known to favor the Bisley model of the Colt single action revolver and his .45 Colt Bisley is in the author's collection. Other Rangers chose the Bisley SAA because of its larger grip frame and improved trigger/hammer action. Named after the Bisley national shooting matches in Great Britain, it was designed to be more accurate and fit the hand better. Despite the target design the Bisley proved to be a popular firearm and period photos can be found of its use on the American frontier. Between the years 1894–1915 Colt produced over 44,000.

Putting aside prohibition, banditry and family feuds there was the threat on the border during the World War I (1914–1918) from foreign invasion. Threats from foreign powers such as Germany and fears from the discovery of the "Plan of San Diego" caused much alarm for South Texas. The lingering threat of an armed Mexican force crossing the border was only magnified when involvement from Germany was discovered. During this World War I period the Texas Ranger force was greatly increased. An unprecedented number of Rangers were funded to help avoid this foreign invasion on our southern border. There is an entire book dedicated to the vast number of Texas Rangers both special and regular Rangers who served during these times. I have a distant relative named Charlie Armstrong who served along the southern border during the World War I years. I have reconstructed his service but he seems to be just one of the many whose records during this time "fell through the cracks." Governor Hobby took office in September 1917. He used the authority of the Home Guard to create eleven new Ranger companies. At full strength (Captain, Sergeant and fourteen privates per companies) the Ranger force would total 175. There never was a foreign invasion on the border, however, Mexican banditry especially in the Big Bend region would continue into the 1920's. On May 21, the infamous Venustiano was killed by an assassin's bullet. One 29 July 1920, Pancho Villa laid down his arms to President Alvaro Obregon and went into retirement. He was destined to also die in an assassination.

The Colt .45 Peacemaker was still the weapon of choice for the Rangers, however, new pistols were making their appearance on the border. The large frame Colt New Service double action revolver was popular south of the border and with some of the Ranger force. It was the revolver of choice for Leon T. Vivian who became a regular Ranger in September 1941. A few others preferred the smaller frame Smith and Wesson military and police model, .38 caliber revolvers. One such Ranger was Gully Cowsert who was Captain in Company E in the late 1940's. He also carried his trusted Colt SAA until his retirement. Almost as popular was the Colt automatic pistol in .45 ACP caliber. It was designed by John Browning and perfected by Sam Colt. It was a seven shot semi-automatic pistol. The first production of the Model 1911 began in January 1912. Most production went to the military but 3,000 commercial pistols were manufactured in 1912. All early models were chambered in .45 ACP caliber until Colt offered the .38 super caliber version in 1929. The .38 super was popular because of its exceptional striking power and range. Less popular, but more desirable as an easily concealable back up weapon, was the Colt model 1908 hammerless in .380 ACP caliber. Also popular for the same reason, was the 1903 hammerless in .32 ACP caliber. These were popular back up weapons and the FBI's number one criminal John Dillinger was carrying a Colt 380 auto at the time of his death.

Again the most popular rifle of the Rangers during this time was the improved Model 1894 lever action carbine. Very limited in usage was the large frame Model 1886, big bore lever action rifle. The Winchester Model 1886 was the improved replacement for the Model 1876 rifle. As previously mentioned the Model 1895 Winchester saw a period of popularity due its part to it being the first early carbines to use high velocity ammunition such as the 30/06 and 30/40 krag. As the ammunition for the Model 1894 became available with improved velocities it again reached the forefront of popularity. As we discussed earlier the popularity the 1894 saw its continued use up until the late 20th century. One of the Rangers I most admire and am honored to call a friend is Retired Ranger H. Joaquin Jackson. His fondness for the 94 carbine is evidenced by including it in his cover photos for his two books One Ranger and One Ranger Returns which are currently in print. The Model 1894 carbine is almost as recognized around the world as the Peacemaker.

CHAPTER 10

ILLUSTRATIONS

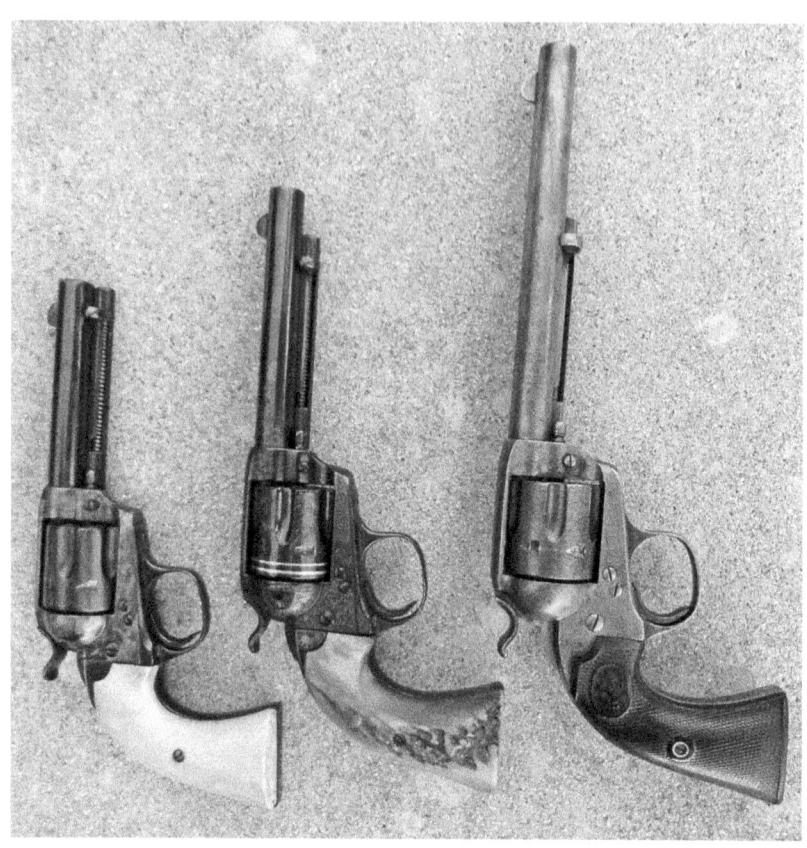

10-1 Colt Bisley Model SAA: *Left*–Bisley model with 4 ¾ inch barrel, 38/40 caliber, mfg 1907. *Middle*–Bisley Model with 5 ½ inch barrel, .45 long colt, engraved with gold inlay on cylinder and elk horn grips, mfg 1906. *Right*–Bisley model 7 ½ inch barrel, .45 long colt mfg 1903. (Author's collection)

10-2 Colt Bisley Model SAA grouping from famous Texas Ranger and Grimes County Sheriff R.M. "Duke" Hudson. .45 long colt 4 ¾ inch barrel, mfg 1906. Duke Hudson joined the Texas Rangers in 1906 in Alpine Texas along with Frank Hamer. (Author's collection)

10-3 Colt Model 1911 automatic pistol: A rare 1912 mfg first year production 1911 .45 ACP. The first year 1911's were the only ones to ever bare the circle Colt stallion stamping on the rear of the slide. (Author's collection)

10-4 Colt 1908 hammerless popular pocket model: automatic in .380 auto caliber, carried by many lawmen as well as law breakers. Example mfg 1928. (Author's collection)

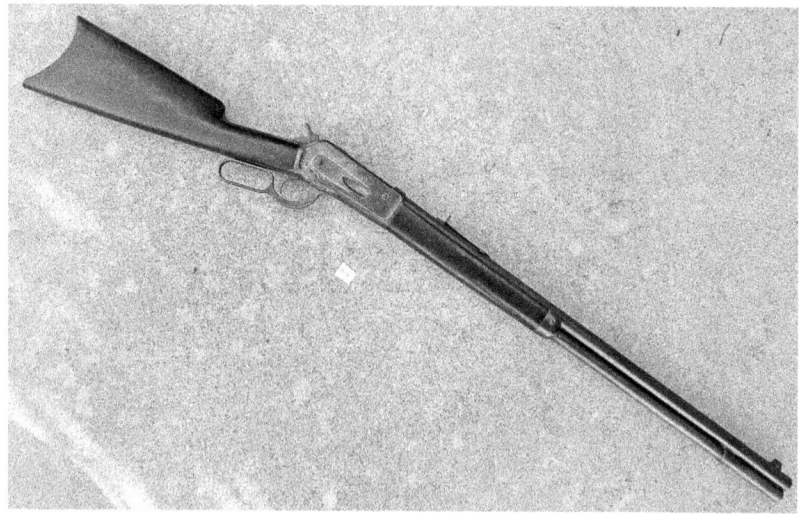

10-5 Winchester Model 1886 rifle: Example in rare .50 express, 50/110 caliber, most desirable of the 1886 calibers and the largest in the Winchester lever action line. Example produced first year in 1887. (Author's collection)

10-6 Winchester Mode 1894 light weight rifle: Special order second year production mfg 1895, with ½ octagon, ½ round and ½ magazine length. (1/2 mag); Shipped 1900. (Author's collection)

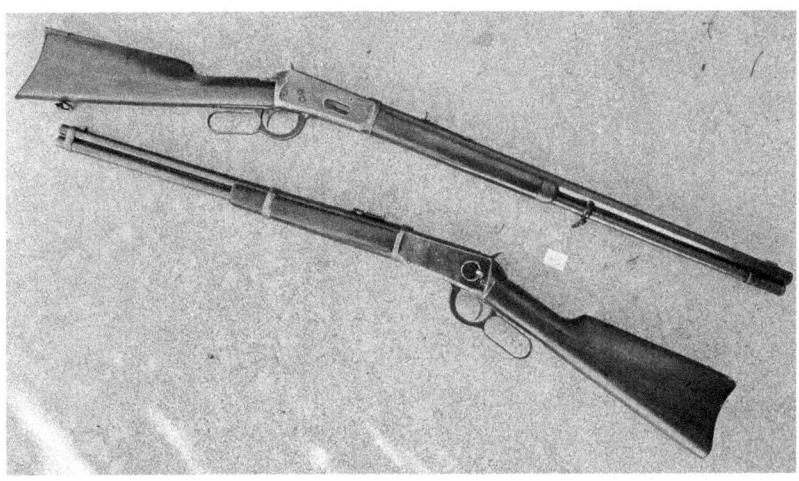

10-7 Winchester Model 1894 rifle and carbine *Top*–octagon 24 inch barrel rifle 30 wcf caliber, second year production mfg 1895. *Bottom*–saddle ring carbine 30/30 caliber mfg 1898. (Author's collection)

10-8 Colt 1878 DA revolver: .45 caliber Colt "Alaskan Model" double action revolver, with 6 inch barrel mfg 1902. Type carried by Henry H. "Hen" Baker. The oversized trigger guard allowed for wearing heavy gloves in winter. Baker was a one-time Texas Ranger and deputy sheriff. He got on the wrong side of the law and was sentenced to Huntsville prison where he murdered another man. He was somehow later given an unconditional pardon and released. He died in Bandera County. (Author's collection)

10-9 Colt Mode 1911 early commercial model: 45 ACP mfg 1917: Slide engraved with name of Charlie Armstrong, Texas Ranger in the date 1918. (Author's collection)

CHAPTER 11

TIME OF THE GANGSTER

Texas didn't experience organized crime such as the mafia in New York City and Chicago but it had its gangsters; those with low regard for human life and the rights of others. These homegrown criminals such as Bonnie Parker and Clyde Barrow dominated the newspapers and radio in the early 1930's. It wasn't until Clyde Barrow in 1934 engineered a successful prison break for his associate and bank robber Raymond Hamilton and three others from the Eastham farm Huntsville prison that his days became numbered. January 15, 1934 the day before the break out, Barrow had hidden two .45 automatic pistols in a culvert near the prison farm's wood yard. In the escape they mortally wounded a prison guard. The director of Texas prisons, Lee Simmons, acquired the services of former Ranger Captain Frank Hamer. His official title was that of Special Prison Investigator. Some believe he was a Texas Ranger at this time but he had previously resigned. He was actually acting under the authority of the highway patrol commission provided through the assistance of the Governor and Warden Simmons. I have seen a copy of the document. As we are more concerned with weapons than events, I can tell you that Bonnie and Clyde carried a small arsenal with them. Clyde favored the 1933-34 Ford Sedan. It was not only stylish with its heart shaped grill and suicide doors but was fast for its time with its flat head V8 Ford engine. The arsenal in the trunk contained such firearms as the Colt 1911, Colt 1908 hammerless, Colt New Service revolver in .45 L/C, Smith and Wesson .38s and a short barrel S&W .38 favored by Bonnie Parker. Long arms carried at times were pump 12 gauge shotguns such as the Remington Model 10 and Winchester 1897. They even used the Winchester lever action 30/30 carbine. They had a virtual gun store on wheels. At the top of their arms list was the Browning automatic rifle or BAR stolen from a Army National Guard Armory. The BAR fired a powerful 30-06 cartridge at a rate of fire of 500/650 rounds per minute. It's reported Clyde sawed off over 6 inches of his BAR barrel—the only time I've known this to be done. State law enforcement agencies at the time were only able to acquire such weapons as the BAR and Thompson Model 1921 submachine gun in limited quantities.

Just a note–As we were talking about Huntsville prison, I had the opportunity to visit with Mr. W.J. "Jim" Estelle, the retired director of the Texas Prison System, in October 2015. I mentioned owning the pistol in illustration 11-5 at the end of the chapter. This pistol was issued to the Texas Prison system at Huntsville, Texas in April 1929. It was used up into the 1970's. Warden Estelle related a story where he inspected the prison arms room and found many over used and unserviceable weap-ons. He instituted a program to replace all obsolete weapons and replaced them with new military surplus weapons, many still wrapped in the ini-tial cosmoline protective wrapping. Director Estelle was a good friend to the Texas Rangers. During our conversation he told me "I never called a Ranger; they just always came." He had the highest respect for the Tex-as Rangers. The W.J. Estelle unit (formally the Ellis II Unit), part of the Huntsville Prison system was named after him and was opened in June 1984

The Thompson invented by General John T. Thompson fired a .45 ACP cartridge so it did not have the devastating power of the BAR. It was favored by the criminal element because of its smaller size and rapid fire power, 600-725 rounds per minute. Now back to Bonnie and Clyde. At the time of their demise Frank Hamer was armed with a Colt Model 1911 automatic in .38 super caliber. This was verified by a modern magazine interview of Hamer's son. It has been mentioned that Capt. Hamer had his trusty SAA Peacemaker with him during the ambush. My speculation is that if this was true it was somewhere in his Ford sedan and not on his person. He had chosen this caliber over his often carried .45 ACP Model 1911 because of the .38 supers increased velocity. He was also known to have been carrying his faithful Remington Model 8 semi automatic rifle in .35 Remington caliber. The Model 8 utilized a long recoil rotating bolt operation. Normally it had a fixed five shot magazine but for police work it had a modified detachable extended magazine. Frank Hamers Model

8 Remington had a customized 15 round magazine purchased from Petmeckeys Sporting Goods Store in Austin, Texas. Captain Hamer is known to have also carried a Model 8, serial number 10045 which was one of two that were utilized in the ambush of Bonnie and Clyde. It had a specially modified 20 round magazine obtained through the Peace Officers Equipment Company of St. Joseph, Missouri. On one occasion Captain Hamer fired his Model 8 at such a high rate that a fellow Ranger referred to it as a "pear burner." The sight of such flame coming from its rifle barrel reminded the Ranger of the gas operated devise used to burn off cactus thorns. A Remington Model 81, a slightly later version of the Model 8 was the DPS issued weapon for Senior Captain Bob Crowder. It is now in the author's collection. One last story about Bonnie Parkers Smith and Wesson .38 revolver as told to me by my good friend and Retired Ranger Johnnie Aycock. The .38 owned and used by Bonnie Parker had been passed down in a family and they offered to give Parkers revolver to him. The only stipulation was that when he was through with it, he would donate it to the Ranger museum under their family name. This unfortunately never came about but what a historical prize it would have been.

Rangers such as Tom Hickman and Manuel T. "Lone Wolf" Gonzaullas policed the boisterous east Texas oil patch when oil was discovered. A number of boom towns sprang up overnight. The task of preserving law and order initially fell to understaffed and under trained local law officers. For a multitude of reasons they fell short. Whether from the lack of resources or just being corrupt the task to keep law and order passed to the Rangers. It's hard to imagine that the primitive conditions in these boom towns left law enforcement to their own devices. With no jail, it was not uncommon to chain prisoners to a convenient tree. "Lone Wolf" Gonzaullas had a unique system of locking prisoners to a common chain; similar to putting fish on a stringer. Gonzaullas favored a Colt Model 1911 .45 ACP pistol. He filed off the trigger guard for easy access. Not one to be outdone, he was big on fancy guns. He owned many examples of engraved and decorated gold and silver inlayed pistols. At the time of his passing he owned a large number of custom pistols. Some are in the Waco Ranger Museum and others in private collections. I always wondered what happened to the remaining vast majority. They still have to be around somewhere, most likely undocumented.

In January 1935, Jimmy Allred became Texas governor. On January 23, 1935 all special ranger commissions were cancelled and all the Ferguson Rangers except three were released from service. New competent Rangers were hired. In 1934 a gun battle in a San Augustine hardware store left four men dead, a vivid reminder of the crime wave in this area. Outgoing Governor Ferguson sent several Ferguson Rangers. True to their nature, nothing was accomplished. Newly elected Governor Allred dispatched Captain McCormick and his Rangers to San Augustine. He ran out any remaining Ferguson Rangers and took head on the two ruthless families with gang ties that were committing robberies, high jacking, forgery, assault, and rape. McCormick roughed up, insulted and through pure strength of force scattered the criminals across the state line to Louisiana. The Ranger force was regaining its reputation lost during the Governor Ferguson years. On August 10, 1935 the department of public safety was created and funded. Captain Tom Hickman became the first Senior Captain in Headquarters Company, Austin under the new DPS structure. Captain Hickman became fed up with all the ongoing politics and only held this position for one year before resigning. Just as a note, I have a Smith and Wesson No. 2 old Army revolver that belonged to Captain Tom Hickman. An interesting fact is that it had a rolled up piece of paper in the barrel. It was a note written in pencil in Tom Hickman's handwriting saying he bought the revolver from Charlie Schreiner III of the Y.O. Ranch, Mountain Home, Texas for $35.00. Most will remember that Charlie Schreiner III was a big supporter of the Texas Rangers. Before his death, he had amassed the largest privately known collection of documented Texas Ranger owned guns. Charlie III as he was known loved the Rangers and they loved him. He was the first major collector to specialize on this type of collection. After his death his collection was auctioned in a big sale held on the west coast. To me it was really a loss that his collection could not have remained intact. It is good however that through his efforts there presently exists a growing number of collectors who specialize in the preservation and documentation of Texas Ranger owned weapons.

CHAPTER 11

ILLUSTRATIONS

11-1 Colt Model 1911s: *Left*–Gangster special This nickel plated .45 automatic with simulated mother of pearl grips was made in 1929. *Right*– First year production (1929) .38 super caliber. This caliber became very popular with law enforcement and Texas Rangers such as Frank Hamer because of it increased velocity. (Author's collection)

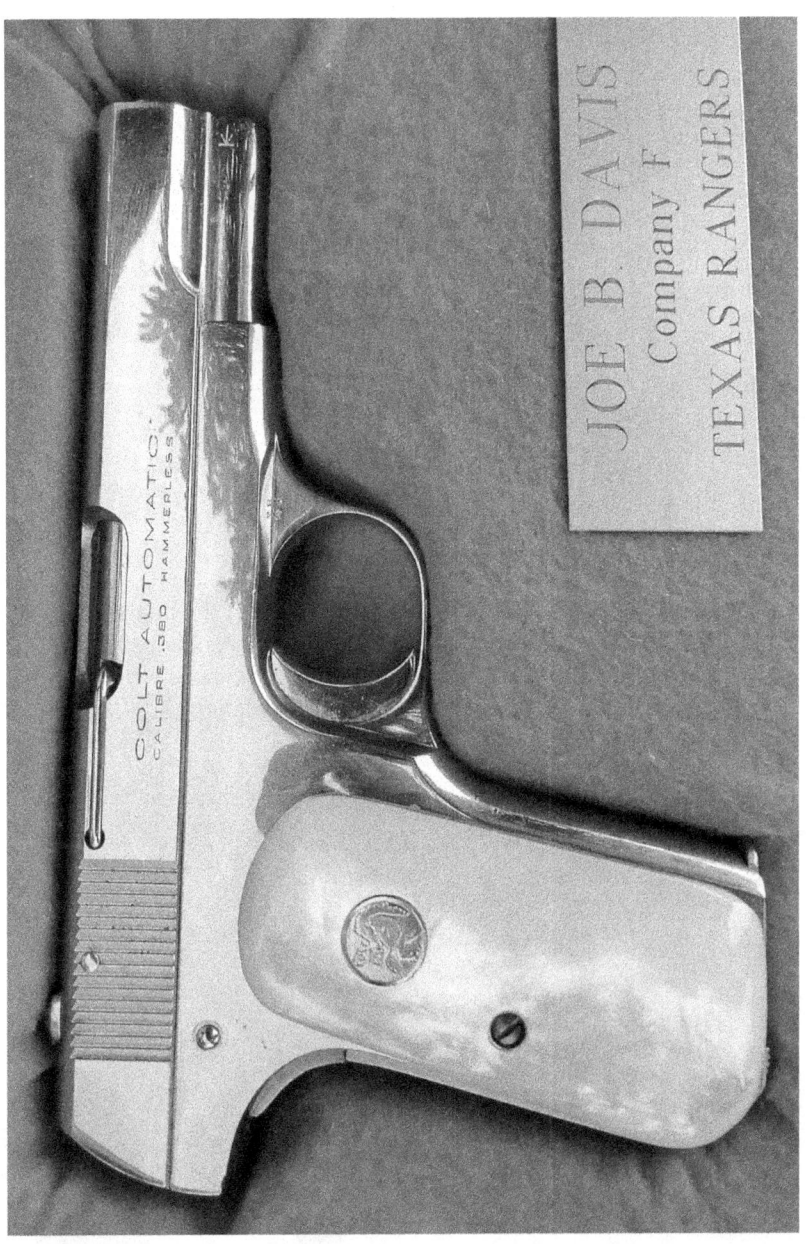

11-2 Colt 380 pocket hammerless automatic Nickel plated .380 caliber with factory mother of pearl grips. Shipped to Wolf and Klar Fort Worth, Texas March 10, 1925. This example belonged to Retired Texas Ranger Joe B. Davis. (Author's collection)

11-3 Winchester Model 1907 semi auto rifle: one of the first semi autos, it was popular with Rangers and local law officers. This example is in .351 Winchester caliber and belonged to the late Texas Ranger Weldon Lucas, B Co. It was manufactured in 1911. (Author's collection)

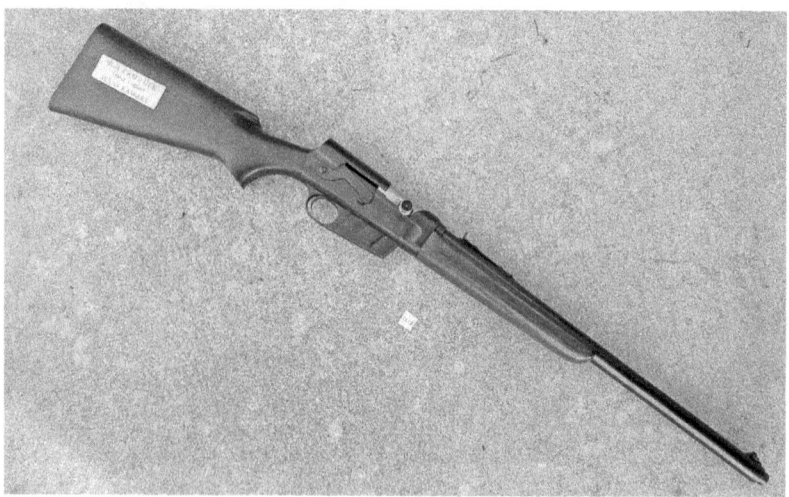

11-4 Remington Model 81 semi auto police rifle: This example was a DPS issue to the late Senior Captain Bob Crowder. It is chambered in .30 Remington caliber and was manufactured in 1939. (Author's collection)

11-5 Smith and Wesson 1st Model: Military and police of 1905 this well used double action nickel plated revolver in .38 special caliber was purchased by the Texas State Prisons. The barrel is marked Texas State Prison and was issued to the Huntsville, Texas prison in April 1929. (Author's collection)

11-6 Colt DA New Army Model revolver .38 special caliber: It is marked Wells Fargo and Company. Colt letter verifies that it was purchased by this company and shipped on 6 December, 1906 as part of a 12 gun shipment. (Author's collection)

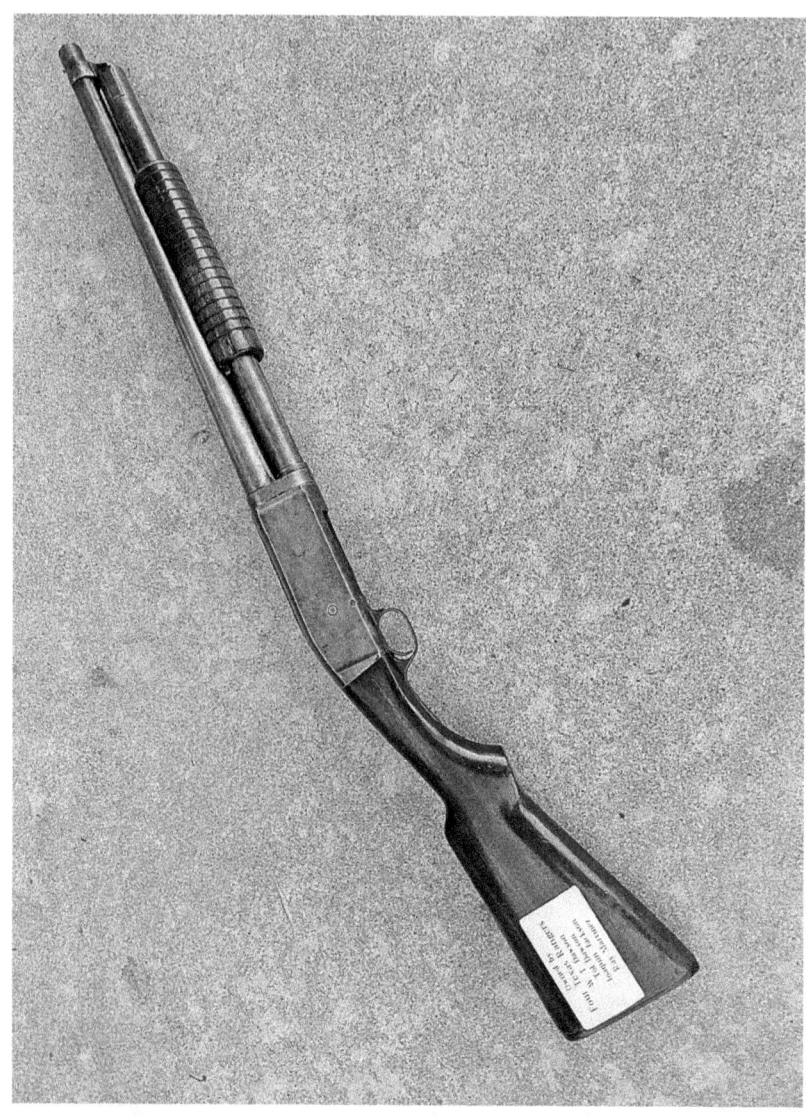

11-7 Remington Model 10A 12 gauge shotgun pump action police configuration manufactured circa 1927: This example at one time belonged to four different Texas Rangers. They were W. T. Dawson, his son Tol Dawson, H. Joaquin Jackson and Ray Martinez. (Author's collection)

CHAPTER 12

POST WW II YEARS

By the close of the 1930's and beginning of the 1940's the major criminal wave had ended. All the key criminals such as Dillinger, Pretty Boy Floyd, Baby Face Nelson, Bonnie and Clyde etc. were either dead or incarcerated. The "high water mark" in criminal activity had been met and things returned to a more normal level. When Japan attacked the United States on 7 December 1941, a state of war existed. Japan had awakened the sleeping giant. By 1942 the industrial manufacturing strength of America was gearing up for full speed. Automobile factories, aircraft factories and yes, firearms manufacturers were dedicating production to support the war effort.

The weapon of choice for the Texas Rangers was still the Colt model 1911 or the improved version 1911 A1. As a side note, the last serving Texas Ranger to give up his Peacemaker as a service weapon was 69 year old Bob Coffee stationed at Sierra Blanca in far west Texas. Colt also suspended war time production of the single action revolver in 1940. These pistols are known as first generation. The second generation Peacemakers date from 1956–1978. The third generation Peacemakers date 1978 to the present. The Colt factory diverted the majority of production to the military to supply the needs of the armed forces. This demand for the 1911 A1 pistol was so great that Colt could not handle the demand alone. It shared the production rights with such companies with Remington Rand, Ithaca, Singer, AJ Savage, Remington UMC, Union Switch and Signal and Springfield Armory. Commercial production of the 1911 A1 stopped in 1942 with serial number C215018. At the close of military production in 1957 the total amount of 1911 A1s manufactured, was 2,695,000.

In 1949 Colt marketed a lightweight 1911 A1 in a reduced size version for the commercial market. It was called the Commander. The Commander model was available in .45 ACP, .38 super and 9mm parabellum calibers. The United States military requirements for the pistol were not established because the ordnance corps decided to suspend the lightweight program. This however, did not prevent its widespread popularity with law enforcement and especially with the Texas Rangers.

One of the military long arms that saw wide spread post war popularity with the Texas Rangers was the M1 .30 caliber carbine. The fully automatic versions were known as the M1A2 and M1A3. In April 1957 on the banks of Walnut Creek, Tarrant County, Capt. Jay Banks used his M3 full automatic version of the US M1 .30 caliber carbine to help end the attempted robbery of the Carswell Air Force Bank. After a high speed car chase, Capt. Banks was instrumental in ending a crime wave of Gene Paul Norris and Carl Humphries in a blaze of automatic gun fire. The M3 carbine was an M1 or M2 carbine with an active infrared scope. The M2 and M3 carbines had a full automatic fire capability. The .30 caliber carbine round was much lighter than the 30/06 in both design and performance. Powerful for its size it fired a round nose 110 gr (7.1 g) bullet. From its 18 inch barrel it produced a muzzle velocity of approximately 1,970 Ft/s (600 m/s).

Retired D Company Ranger H. Joaquin Jackson on 3 April, 1969 used his M2 .30 caliber M1 carbine in full automatic mode during the standoff and attempted jail break at the Dimmit County jail in Carrizo Springs. Together with the heroism of the late Capt Alfred Y. Allee Sr. and the late Ranger Tol Dawson, the jail break was prevented. Speaking about automatic weapons if I could go back in time to the early 1920s for one of the first uses of the Thompson Model 1921 submachine gun. We discussed the Thompson 45 ACP submachine gun in an earlier chapter. Texas Rangers Tom Hickman and Frank Hamer accompanied by 15 other Rangers made a raid on the notorious joints (Winter Garden and Chicken Ranch). They were armed with 12 gauge "scatter guns" and the new 45 ACP Thompsons. The use of the new Thompson proved highly successful in opening the door to a new era in law enforcement. Pump action 12 gauge shotguns firing the 00 (double ought) buckshot were still the standard issue and one could be found in every Ranger's automobile trunk. Also included were a high power rifle, radio, first aid kit, ammunition and other items needed in emergency or survival situations. There is a picture of a 1970s vintage police sedan with Capt W.D. Wilson and Ranger Joe B. Davis standing alongside it. Laid out on the ground as if ready for military inspections were all the essential weapons, ammunition and support equipment needed to accompany the Rangers of this era. The automobile trunk housed all the things needed for their home away from home. It was not unusual for a Ranger to live out of his automobile when deeply involved in an investigation.

The first elected DPS director was Horace H. Carmichael in 1936. He replaced Highway Patrol Chief Louis G. Phares who was acting director. Carmichael was a dedicated man and straightened out the existing difficulties between the Highway patrol and Ranger divisions. Unfortunately his tenure was cut short by a heart attack while driving in Austin on September 24, 1938. Director Carmichael purchased a Colt match target bulls eye woodsman .22 caliber pistol in 1938 from Zork Hardware Company, El Paso, Texas. This special order pistol was shipped in August 1938 and was sent directly to Camp Perry, Ohio to be used by the Texas State pistol team during the 1938 Camp Perry national shooting matches. Replacing director Carmichael was his deputy director Homer Garrison. He took over in 1938. Colonel Garrison did more to foster the professional image of the Ranger force than any director since or after his time in office. He influenced the day to day activities of the Rangers to such an extent that those who served during his tenure were known as Garrison Rangers.

During the 1960s through 1990s the Rangers continue to serve as the top of the ladder law enforcement force in Texas. High profile crime events such as "the Kentucky Fried Chicken" murders, the trial of George Parr and bringing order to Duval County as well as the 1974 Huntsville prison seizure of the third floor Walls unit by Federico Gomez Carrasco challenged the Rangers. Also during this time Rangers had to deal with the Amy McNeal and the Kara Leigh Whitehead kidnappings. The Henry Lee Lucas investigations dominated much of the Rangers time and caused great frustration in the law enforcement community.

During this time firearms technology changed very little. Rangers were still carrying the Colt 1911s and a few preferred the Browning high power in 9mm caliber. The Department of Public Safety believed in the .357 magnum revolvers and I was fortunate to acquire the Smith & Wesson model 586 and "blue card," the DPS inventory record for the service weapon issued to Sr. Capt. Bruce Casteel. It is an honor to know Bruce. He is not only a well respected professional retired Texas Ranger, but a true gentleman.

The Winchesters both lever action and semi automatic versions and the Remington semi-automatic rifles were slow to be phased out of the DPS inventory. If they got the job done, they remained in inventory. With the war in Viet Nam proving the effectiveness of the AR15 and M16 series, it was just a matter of time before they became standard issue to the Rangers. The early AR-15 flat side version of the M-16 was popular and a photograph from the Amy McNeal kidnapping in 1985 shows B Company Ranger Brantley Foster holding his AR-15 at the conclusion and capture of the criminals involved. Amy McNeal was released unharmed and is now a wife and mother. Her brother who was present at the initial abduction of his sister Amy is said to currently be a Texas Highway Patrol officer. Beside the various M-16 versions used, the Ruger mini-14 was also a DPS service weapon, although there were many who felt the mini-14 fell short on its capabilities.

I have stopped my story telling at the 1990s for one, that my knowledge base stops here and secondly, the modern weapons lack the mystique, class and collectability of the older models. The currently used Glocks and Sig firearms are to me just ugly lusterless weapons. I know they are highly dependable and accurate. You can drop them in the mud, shake them off and keep firing. This is great and I know many modern law enforcement officers swear by them, but I guess I am just a traditionalist at heart. There is just something about a Colt 1911 with elephant ivory grips that just speaks class. The modern Rangers have the option to choose their service carry pistol and many prefer the Sig 226 or similar weapon. As times change a need exists for more accurate and dependable firearms, but there's just something about a Colt 1911 in the hands of a Ranger from the 20th century that brings glorious memories of bygone days.

CHAPTER 12

ILLUSTRATIONS

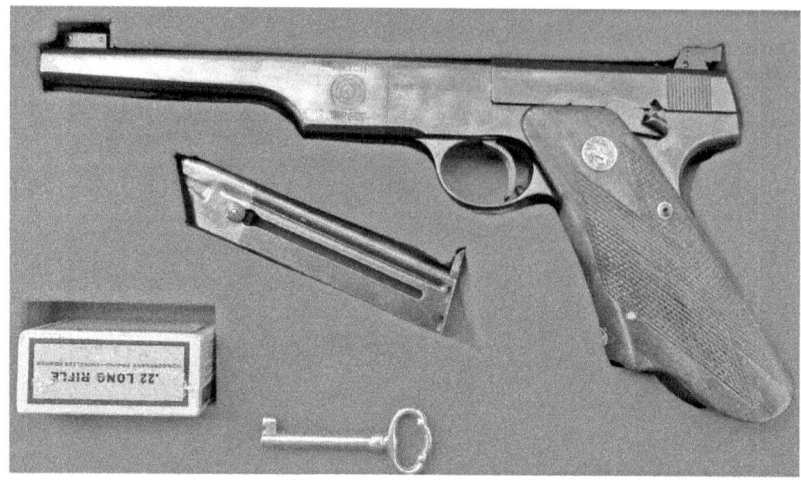

12-1 Colt Woodsman .22 national match: Known as Bulls Eye Model, this first year first model special order pistol was ordered by the late DPS director Horace H. Carmichael. Colt letter shows he purchased it from Zork Hardware, El Paso and it was shipped 12 August, 1938 to Camp Perry, Ohio for the state national pistol championships. (Author's collection)

12-2 Smith & Wesson Model 586 .357 magnum revolver: This revolver was DPS issued service weapon for Sr. Capt Bruce Casteel. Blue Card shows issue on 1 September 1992. (Author's collection)

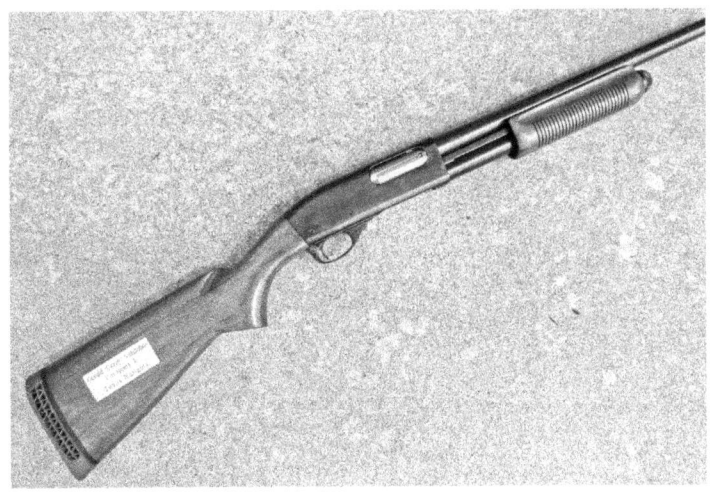

12-3 Remington pump 870 police shotgun: 12 gauge DPS issue this 870 Wingmaster shotgun was purchased from a DPS surplus auction by Texas Ranger Gerald Villalobos, Sgt Retired Company E. (Author's collection)

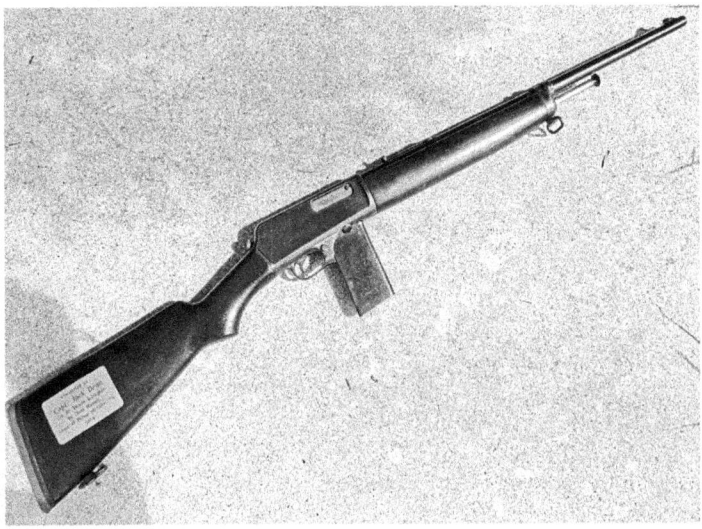

12-4 Winchester Model 1907 semi loader: .351 Winchester caliber police rifle as owned by Texas Ranger Capt and US Marshall Jack Dean. I had the opportunity to speak with Jack on this rifle at a 2015 Waco Texas Ranger get together. He remembers it vividly and said it was given to his wife by the former Chief of police Clint Mussey of McAllen, Texas in 1974. (Author's collection)

12-5 Smith & Wesson pre model 10 revolver: 2 inch barrel .38 special; this revolver was the DPS issue in 1952 assigned by blue card to DPS Capt Hugh Shaw. As Captains and above could choose to carry 2 inch barrel revolvers Capt Shaw carried this revolver until his retirement in 1978. Texas Ranger Gerald A. Villalobos who also served as a state trooper under Capt. Shaw purchased it from a DPS auction. (Author's collection)

12-6 Remington M81 DPS issue to Byron Currin Texas Ranger Co. C 1955 - 1973. (Author's collection)

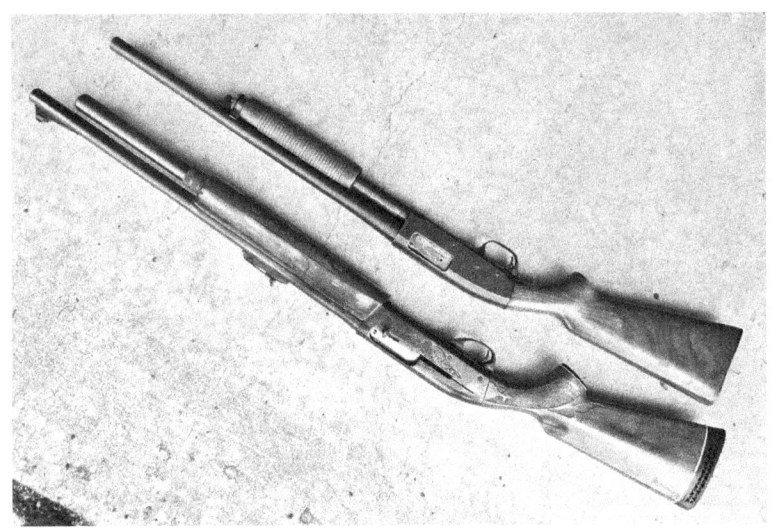

12-7 Remington 12 ga. DPS issue shotguns, pump model called "Captains Gun" owned by Retired Major Ret. Dewayne Dockery. Semi-automatic mode issued to three Rangers, A.L. Mitchell, Joe Coleman, and Lt. Jim Denman who purchased it on 03/28, 2007 when it retired from DPS. (Author's collection)

12-8 M4 Carbine, M16 family: Example of current M4 carbine configuration. Most often found in .223 caliber, The M4 evolved from the Car 15 part of the AR 15 family and evolved into the M16 as we know it today. (Author's collection)

12-9 US Army 1911 A1: WWII production Remington Rand manufactured 1943 .45 ACP. Fully engraved with gold inlaid Celtic symbols with carved oversized ivory grips–engraved by Master Engraver Sean McVicker, Stories in Steel. (Author's collection)

12-10 Colt lightweight Commander: .45 ACP, two tone early lightweight 1911 A1 Commander, carved elephant ivory grips with Colt Rampant Stallion. Mfg 1950. (Author's collection)

CHAPTER 13

BAR-B-Q GUNS

When I hear the term Bar-B-Q, I have images of outdoor picnics, smoked brisket and festive activities. When it comes to pistols and the Rangers, the term Bar-B-Q guns brings to mind a fancy pistol sometimes engraved with ivory or mother of pearl grips. I'm not sure where the term originated but many Rangers have had a bit of showman in them.

One of the first to like to "show off" was W.W. Bill Sterling. He came from a south Texas ranching family and served as a Cap-tain of Texas Rangers. He also served as Texas Adjutant General in the early 1930's under Governor Sterling, no relationship. He headed numerous rodeos and public events wearing his fancy pistol belt and engraved Colt 6 shooter. Tom Hickman who was a Texas Ranger Captain also served as the first Senior Captain under the 1935 Department of Public Safety organization. Tom was also a bit of a showman and loved to rodeo. There are numerous 1930's vintage pictures with him in his fancy western garb and flashy six gun. Tom Hickman resigned after one year as Senior Captain but came back in the early 1960's to lead the three man public safety commission. He was chairman of the commission when he died in 1962. Manuel T. "Lone Wolf" Gonzaullas served as a Ranger and federal prohibition agent during the 1920's and 1930's. He was Captain of Company B in 1940 through 1951. Referred to as flashy and vain, he was also regarded as one of the very finest Rangers of his time. He loved his fancy engraved pistols and even went as far as to design jewel encrusted pistol grips with silver and gold inlays. He mounted a Thompson 45 ACP submachine gun on his armored 1932 Chrysler. This talks volumes about his persona.

Captains Jay Banks and Bob Crowder carried fancy pistols. Jay Banks liked his double action engraved Model 19 S & W revolver with stag horn grips. Bob Crowder liked to wear a tooled leather holster set up with two .45 automatic 1911's. When Captain Crowder put down the riot in the maximum security unit of the Rusk State Hospital in April 1955, he was carrying two .45 autos. Vainer than most Ranger Captains and with an ego as big as Waco was Clint Peoples. He served as Senior Captain from 1969 to 1973 and later served as a US Marshall for the Northern District of Texas. He was instrumental in founding the Waco Texas Ranger Museum. He was a showman of modern times and loved his fancy guns. Many of his custom engraved pistols are in private collections. He was known to sell numerous pistols that he claimed to have carried to supplement his income. An engraved example of one of his Colt 1911 A1 com-manders is illustrated in this chapter. My late mother who was good friends with Captain Peoples obtained this pistol for me many years ago.

Even the well respected director of public safety, Colonel Homer Garrison liked his moment of flash. He served as director from 1938 until 1968. There is a vintage 1930's photograph of Colonel Garrison with fancy cowboy boots, pants tucked in, a fancy 2 gun tooled leather pistol rig with two engraved Colt single action army revolvers. He was also known to carry a matched pair of engraved Colt model 1911's with silver and gold grips. Like Horace Carmichael, the director before him, Garrison considered himself a Ranger. He also had Ranger Captains report directly to him.

Charlie Miller who served on and off as a Texas Ranger from 1919 through 1968 had his retirement party at the Y.O. Ranch in

June 30, 1968. He liked to carry his Bar-B-Q gun, a Colt 1911 with initialed ivory grips with an unusual raised metal embossed leaf and vine pattern. Charlie believed in tying down the grip safety so it was always ready to fire. Jim Nance a well respected Ranger served his time in Sierra Blanca in far west Texas (Born 1899 died 1971) He had a 4 ¾ inch barrel SAA engraved with silver engraved grips for special occasions. One of his regular peacemakers is illustrated in this chapter. Also illustrated in this chapter is an engraved 1911 A1 that was carried by retired Captain "Dino" Henderson of Headquarters Company, Austin where he retired in 2014.

The Texas Ranger Museum and Hall of Fame located in Waco, Texas has many interesting and historical engraved Texas Ranger owned weapons. If you haven't visited them, I highly recommend you make the trip. It is a pleasant learning experience for the whole family. I am presently involved with the new Texas Ranger Heritage Center located adjacent to historical Fort Martin Scott in Fredericksburg, Texas. At the time of this writing, phase one of construction is completed and phase two is to begin at an unspecified time. At whatever year it is completed, it will be a real asset to Texas and the historical preservation of the Texas Rangers.

I have casually talked with numerous Department of Public Safety officers about the fancy engraved Colts of past time. I was told by the uniform officers that they are required to carry the DPS service provided pistols. Modern day Rangers have more latitude and are permitted to carry a hand gun of choice although many choose the department provided Sig 226 or similar tactical pistols. As times change the technology requirements change and the vanity of wearing any engraved "Bar-B-Q" pistol seems less important. It may be an obsolete feeling but the fancy pistols carried on special occasions by early Texas Rangers recall a glorious image of a noble Western lawman. This image of a frontier lawman wearing his Ranger scout tooled leather pistol belt with silver buckle set holstering an impressive pistol with ivory or silver grips and wearing his gray

Stetson hat is imbedded in the minds of traditional historians. Well, we still have the hat and we still have the character of the Rangers. They still have the courage and devotion of the Rangers who have gone before them. As director Homer Garrison stated," the Rangers may change but the character remains the same."

CHAPTER 13

ILLUSTRATIONS

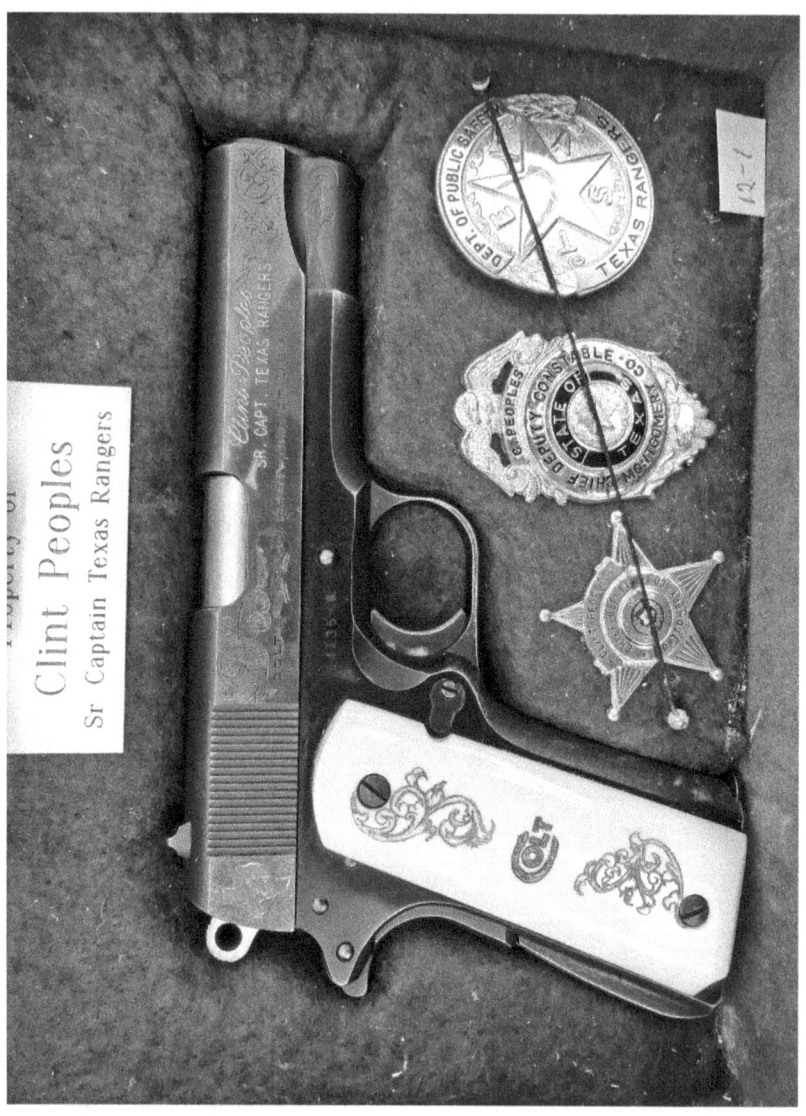

13-1 Colt lightweight Commander: Early lightweight commander in .45 ACP, owned and carried by Sr. Capt. Clint Peoples. Slide engraved with his name and Texas flag and badge with vintage ivory grips. Badges were three worn by Capt. Peoples, mfg 1951. (Author's collection)

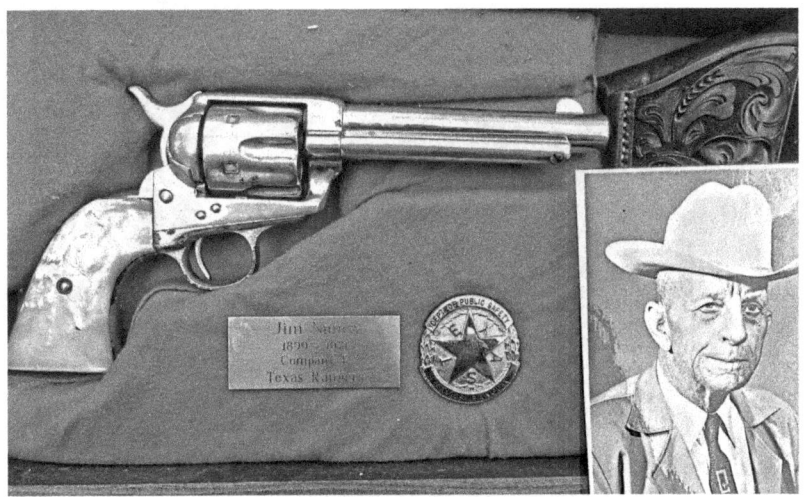

13-2 Colt single action army .45 L/C mfg 1884: Nickel plated with mother of pearl grips, this peacemaker was owned by Texas Ranger Jim Nance Company E, Sierra Blanca–served 1953 to 1969. Jim died in August 1971. (Author's collection)

13-3 Colt python .357 magnum: one of two specially ordered presentation Colt pythons. Custom engraved by the Master engraver at Halthom City Jewelers. One presented to Clint Peoples who at the time was serving as US Marshall Northern District of Texas and the other to his chief deputy, Jim Conrad. Example was presented to Deputy Marshall Conrad. (Author's collection)

13-4 1911 A1 US Army Remington Rand (1943): Fully engraved WW2 contract model 1911 A1 owned and carried by Capt. Howard D. "Dino" Henderson Headquarters Company, Austin. He retired in April 2014. (Author's collection)

13-5 Colt 1911 US Army mfg 1918: Fully engraved with 24 carat gold inlays on the slide one of tiger and one of elk. Mexican gold and coin silver grips fitted with target sights. (Author's collection)

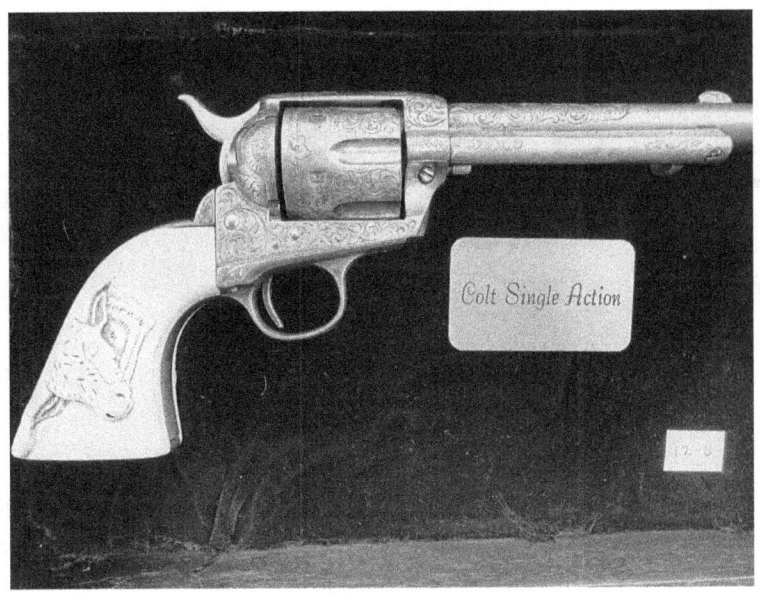

13-6 Colt SAA 5 ½ inch bbl 38/40 wcf: Early engraving in the LD Nimschke style, sterling silver platted finish, hand carved steer head ivory grips, mfg 1906. (Author's collection)

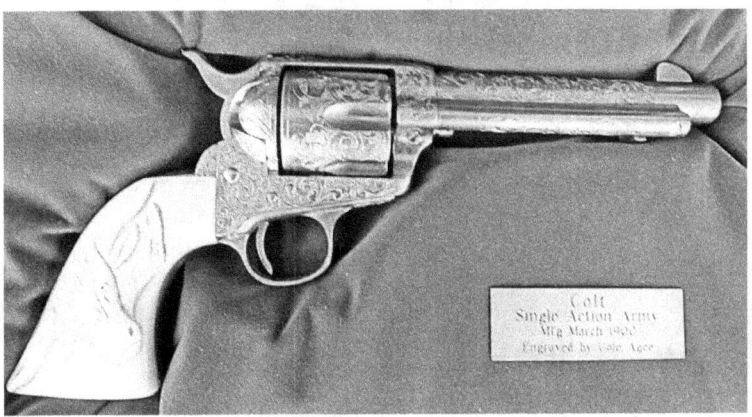

13-7 Colt SAA 5 ½ inch bbl 45 long colt: Single action army revolver engraved by the late and famous Cole Agee who is credited with inventing the cattle brand style of engraving, carved mother of pearl grips. Example mgf 1900. (Author's collection)

13-8 Colt SAA 4 ¾ inch bbl 38/40 long colt: Deep custom engraving in the cattle brand style by David W. Harris. Hand carved aged ivory steer head grips. Mfg 1904. (Author's collection)

13-9 Ruger Vaquero Sheriffs model: Engraved sheriffs model, 3 ¾ inch barrel, 45 Colt caliber, engraved by Peter D. Maskunas, Sgt Co A Retired. (Author's collection)

CHAPTER 14

COMMEMORATIVES AND SPECIAL EDITION FIREARMS

Gun collectors are as varied in taste as anyone. There are collectors who specialize in one make of weapon, others in specific calibers and those specific purpose such as U.S. military or law enforcement. In the 1960's and 1970's another type of collector emerged. One who specializes not in a particular model or design but in a style called a commemorative. They are defined as a firearm manufactured for the sole purpose of honoring a person, place or event. It all started in 1961 when Robert Cherry, Geneseo, Illinois contacted Colt to produce a limited number of .22 short, 4th model derringers. The idea started slow but soon began to snowball. Colt issued a special grade 125th anniversary Colt SAA to celebrate the firms 125th year. Marlin issued a 90th anniversary model 39-A rifle and carbine. It was then that some states decided that a nice hand gun or rifle suitably decorated would make an ideal commemorative for their centennial or sesquicentennial celebrations. As the number of commemoratives increased, people began to collect them. Some with an eye toward investment others began to collect them as a tangible reminder of a historical event.

Simply stamping some dates and adding a bit of etching to an otherwise standard production arm doesn't make it a commemorative. It must have top shelf stocks, finish and workmanship of the highest quality. Colt industries have produced the largest number of commemoratives. More than 11 other U.S. arms manufacturers have issued one or more. Leading as the manufacturer producing the majority of these long arms is Winchester. Others include Marlin, High Standard, Ithaca, Ruger, Smith & Wesson, Remington and the list goes on.

In the same category as the commemoratives are the limited or special edition firearms. The Colt custom shop is still producing these firearms on a special order basis. There are a number of Colt commemoratives and limited edition pistols that were produced and offered for sale by private companies to celebrate an event of their choosing. Investment values are often soft with the value being less than the purchase price. For those who enjoy collecting these firearms without investment goals these private commemoratives offer an additional outlet. There are literally hundreds of special and limited edition firearms on the open markets. I will only further mention the ones that pertain to the Texas Ranger.

One of the most currently encountered Texas Ranger commemoratives is the Smith & Wesson Model 19-3, .357 magnum revolver with 4 inch barrel. This is most often accompanied by a matching Ranger Bowie knife and encased in a walnut display case. This boxed set was released in 1973 and there were a total of 10,000 produced. The original selling price was $250.00. Of this total number, 50 were said to be engraved by the Smith & Wesson factory engraver, Tom Fryburger. Today these engraved boxed sets bring a much greater price. Bond Arms produces a current two barrel Derringer they call the 200th Anniversary Model (1823–2023). It is a .45 Colt/410 shotgun combination with gold embossed "Texas Rangers" on the side. Beretta offered in the past, a limited edition Texas Ranger Model 92. Serial numbering was based on the Rangers' seniority within the force. It was only offered to serving Rangers and not the commercial market. Sig Sauer Arms offered a Model 220 .45 ACP pistol with blue finish and gold accents. Pistol again was offered to serving Rangers. A total of 173 were released and serial numbers were based on seniority. Sig also released a Model 1911 Texas Ranger Special Edition in 2011 to celebrate 100 years of the Model 1911. It was offered only to serving Rangers and the slides were factory marked with the Rangers name, badge and company. Colt also released a series of single action revolvers especially serial numbered to the serving Rangers at the time. There has been numerous Colt versions of the model 1911 released to commemorate Ranger service. One recent release and one near and dear to my heart is the Colt Combat Commander, Former Texas Ranger Foundation pistol in .38 super. It is sometimes referred to as the "Directors Model" as it was basically available only to those in advisory or leadership positions within the Foundation. The total marketed was initially only 54 but I have later heard of totals as high as 76. It is possible that the 76 was the target number for initial procurement. The FTRF board convinced Lt. Gen. Keyes, CEO Colt Industries, to produce through the Colt custom shop this limited one time offering. There was only a three week window to purchase these Colts. An example of the FTRF Colt .38 super is includ-ed in this chapters illustrations. The FTRF released a Colt custom shop M1911A1 series 70, government sized commemorative in .45 ACP to honor 45 years of the foundation. Less than 100 were released and mem-bers who acquired the first FTRF commemorative in .38 Super were offered the new pistols with the same serial numbers. I was fortunate to get serial #12 in each model.

The n ext T exas R anger c ommemorative w e'll d iscuss i s o ne o f the prime examples of modern day Ranger heritage. In the late 1960's Charles Schreiner III, who came from a Ranger family and was a big supporter and collector of Texas Ranger firearms, obtained permission from the Department of Public Safety to have Colt produce 1,000 single action Army revolvers honoring the Texas Rangers. Serial numbering ranged from 1–1,000, each ending with "T*R." A limited number were offered engraved with ivory grips. The majority were sold in a walnut 2 drawer display case but could also be obtained with just the Colt factory paper box. These Colts have become highly collectable due in part to the involvement and subsequent fame of the late Charlie Schreiner III and the Y.O. Ranch in Mountain Home, Texas. There is even an offering from a Texas museum for a Texas Ranger tribute .45 ACP Thompson 1927 A-1 with drum magazine. If he were alive, "Lone Wolf" Gonzaullas would have wanted one of these.

I could go on and on about the different offerings of special edition weapons, but I think I will stop here. You get the idea. There are plenty to choose from. Just keep in mind when collecting these type pistols and rifles that condition is everything. The original condition of the factory box is important as is the condition of the weapon itself. Some buyers even go as far as to say "The cylinder has never been turned." This is going a little far for me, but the point is, the less a commemorative is handled, the more its worth at resale. Obviously you don't want to fire one if you are concerned with resale value. Again as I stated earlier I am a traditionalist. I like to pick something up and imagine its history, who carried the pistol or rifle and what could it tell us if it could talk. This is why I like the real deal. Original historical firearms carry with them a mystique that doesn't exist with modern commercial weapons. There is a place for newly manufactured commemoratives and I personally have a few that are important to me, however, what really gets my heart pumping is the pistols and rifles of the 19th and 20th centuries and most especially the ones owned and carried by our Texas Rangers.

One last topic in this chapter concerns a category of collecting not previously covered. It is the collectability of previously owned and documented Texas Ranger guns. This is a challenging field as the offering is very limited. Only on a rare occasion do you find a documented i.e. letter from Ranger or qualified family member stating the provenance. Many retired Rangers are unwilling to sell and document one of their personal firearms for fear it will end up some place that might be an embarrassment. This could be an internet auction or crime scene. A Ranger weapon is an extension of his persona. It is understandable that they would be cautious as to who ended up with them. Because of those concerns, the selling price for a documented gun can be from 100 to 400% over the value of the gun alone. The value is also influenced by the type of weapon, the service record, and name recognition of the Ranger. I can't fault a retired Ranger trying to supplement their retirement and I can also understand their reservations to transfer a firearm without confidence in its final disposition. Personally my Ranger guns are very special to me. I treat them with the respect and dignity that the Ranger would expect. At my age, I know I can't take them with me when I pass on to a better place, but I can ensure that while I'm here, they will be protected.

CHAPTER 14

ILLUSTRATIONS

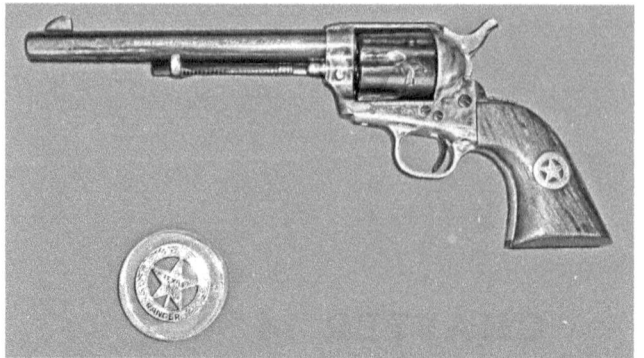

14-1 Charlie Schreiner III Texas commemorative: Cased Colt SAA 45/C 7 ½ inch barrel with matching cowhide covered book, pictorial history of the Texas Rangers. Book serial numbered to the gun also included is a Texas Ranger badge made from a Mexican peso coin. Mfg 1969. (Author's collection)

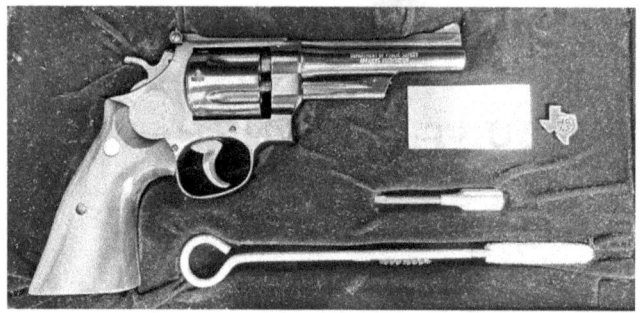

14-2 Smith & Wesson Model 27-2: 357 Magnum revolver DPSOA owned by the late Texas Ranger and Denton County Sheriff, Weldon Lucas. Weldon died on 5 January, 2011 after 41 years in law enforcement. Example represents the Department of Public Safety Officers Association (DPSOA) Model. (Author's collection)

14-3 Photograph B Company Texas Ranger Weldon Lucas: photo from 1980's shows Texas Ranger Weldon Lucas and the serial killer Henry Lee Lucas while investigating possible murder sights. (Author's collection)

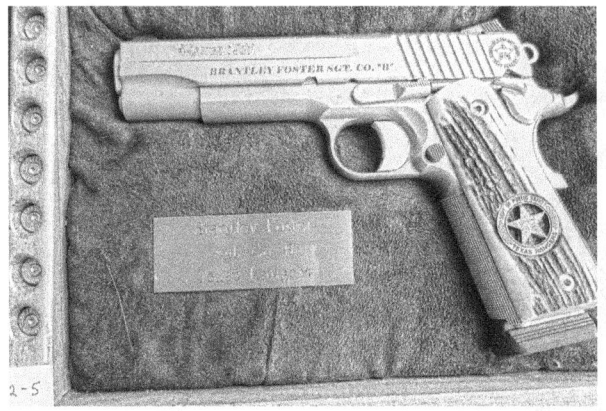

14-4 Sig Sauer Special Configuration Model 1911: 1911 Texas Ranger Model, 300 produced and could be ordered with the Rangers name and company. Illustration has the slide factory personalized to Sgt. Brantley Foster, B Company. (Author's collection)

14-5 FTRF Special Edition Colt Commander: Former Texas Rangers Foundation .38 super Commander. Example mfg 2013 and is serial numbered FTRF O12, the 12th Colt produced in this series of 54. (Author's collection)

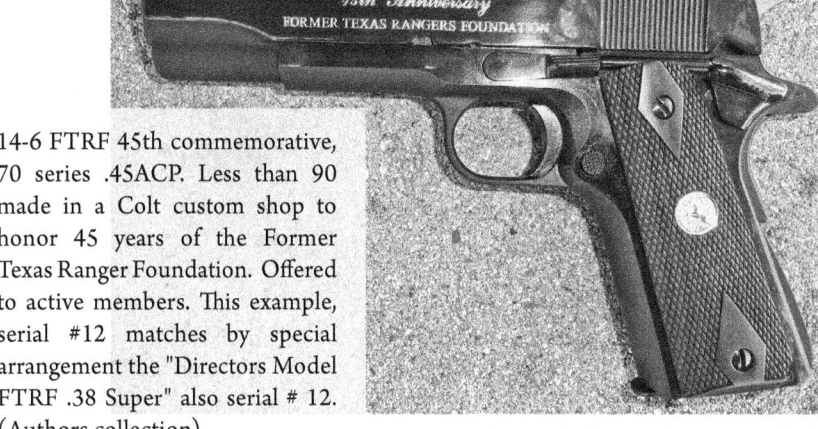

14-6 FTRF 45th commemorative, 70 series .45ACP. Less than 90 made in a Colt custom shop to honor 45 years of the Former Texas Ranger Foundation. Offered to active members. This example, serial #12 matches by special arrangement the "Directors Model FTRF .38 Super" also serial # 12. (Authors collection)

14-7 175th Commemorative Texas Rangers sold left and right pairs, shipped to Texas Ranger Steve Foster

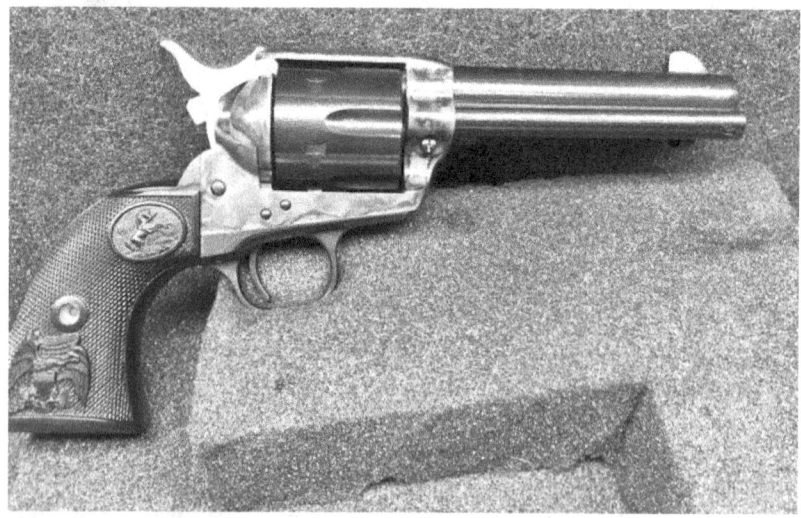

14-8 Texas Ranger Single Action Army, .45LC, unusual that it is not a commemorative but was made and offered to each of the 94 serving Texas Rangers in 1984. This example belonged to Ranger Calvin J. (Buster) Collins. This limited series has become highly collectable. (Authors collection)

CHAPTER 15

FAVORITES

One of my favorite guns is not the expected engraved Colt with ivory grips. It is in fact a very simple Taurus PT 1911 in .45 ACP. What makes it so special is that it was owned and carried by the Honored Texas Ranger and my good friend Johnnie Aycock. I had the slide personalized with his name and "Texas Ranger." For anyone who doesn't know of Johnnie Aycock, he is very humble. He would be the last to tell you about his accomplishments as a Texas Ranger. I've been the one to brag on him and at times he hasn't appreciated it. However, he deserves all the praise that may come his way. Example, the DPS Medal of Valor has only been awarded 5 times to a Texas Ranger and Johnnie was recipient two of these five times. His picture is inside the Waco Texas Ranger Museum in the circular Walk of Fame where there are two Medals of Valor next to his picture. He was never a desk Ranger. He has been in more shootouts than I have fingers. He was awarded his medals when he successfully brought to conclusion two different child kidnappings, one involving the tragic death of one of his fellow Rangers. For this Johnnie made the kidnapper pay the ultimate price. This is all a matter of public record and the events are in numerous Texas Range history books. This Taurus is pictured in the illustrations of this chapter along with a Winchester Model 94 carbine also used by Johnnie. What is also interesting about this Taurus PT 1911 is that Johnnie had Herman Mueschke of Houston, Texas fine tune this pistol and add custom made ambidextrous safeties. Herman Mueschke was a long time friend of the Texas Rangers over the years. In 2005 Senior Captain Earl Pearson appointed him the "Official Armorer" of the

Texas Rangers. Hermen built many 1911s, and .45 autos for Rangers over the state and worked on modified guns for them over the years. He passed away on September 17, 2015 and he will be deeply missed.

Another of my favorites is a Colt Commander 45 ACP with a Texas Ranger Star carved into the right grip with the name Joaquin Jackson. I acquired this Colt from Joaquin while a guest in his home in Alpine, Texas. He is a good friend and a great Texas Ranger. I have been a big fan of Joaquin's ever since I first saw the 1987 movie "Extreme Prejudice" with Nick Nolte and Powers Booth. Nolte portrayed a fictitious Texas Ranger named Jack Benteen whose character was based on Joaquin who also served as the technical advisor on the movie. Most recently he served as technical advisor to Jeff Bridges on how to act as a Ranger in the 2016 motion picture *Hell or High Water*. Joaquin just looks like a Ranger ought to: tall, muscular with an authoritative air. He is pictured on the cover of his 2 books holding one of his favorite Winchester carbines. If you read his book, which I highly recommend, you will find he is no Hollywood Ranger. He served with destination along the Mexican border and was directly involved with the successful conclusion of numerous high profile criminal cases. He has devoted many hours to fund raisers and special events to better promote and preserve the image and history of the Texas Rangers. I value every moment I have been able to spend with Joaquin. He is a true American hero and a "Texas Rangers' Ranger.

In conclusion to this book I have tried to touch briefly the subject of the specific type or pistols and rifles carried by the Texas Rangers over their time in existence. It is in no way a comprehensive study but rather a light history in the story tellers' fashion.

I have tried to cover a number of time periods and have highlighted a few historical events for the purpose of clarifying the time period. There are vast selections of books on the history of the Texas Rangers. I have tried to make this one different by making the firearms the central subject and not the specific Ranger or event. It has been a fun journey for me and hope it will be enjoyed by the readers.

CHAPTER 15

ILLUSTRATIONS

15-1 Taurus PT 1911 .45 ACP automatic government model: This pistol was tuned and new ambidextrous safeties installed by the Texas Ranger armorer Herman Mueschke of Houston, Texas. This pistol owned and carried by Texas Ranger Johnnie Aycock, Co F retired. (Author's collection)

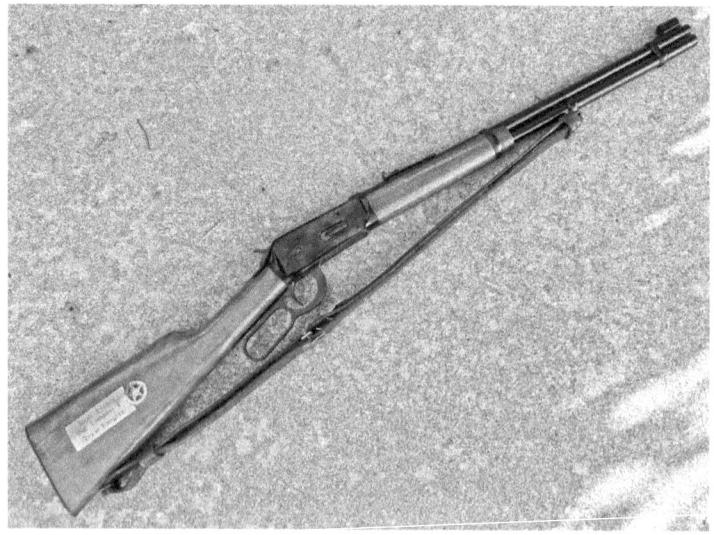

15-2 Winchester Model 1894 Lever action 30/30 carbine: Owned and carried by Retired Texas Ranger Johnnie Aycock. Mfg circa 1966. (Author's collection)

15-3 Photo Johnnie Aycock: photograph of retired Texas Ranger Johnnie Acycock and the author at the Former Texas Ranger Association 2015 annual meeting at Fredericksburg, Texas. (Author's photo)

15-4 Colt Lightweight Commander .45 ACP: Early lightweight commander with custom ivory grips with badge carved in right grip with the name of "Texas Ranger Joaquin Jackson." Pistol owned and carried by Ranger Jackson. (Author's collection)

15-5 Engraved lightweight engraved Commander: Early Colt Lightweight Commander, .45 ACP custom engraved for Retired Texas Ranger H. Joaquin Jackson. Engraving by Master Engraver Shawn McVicker, Stories in Steel. It has Mexican gold and silver grips. Author had this Colt specifically engraved for Joaquin. (Author's photo)

15-6 Picture of H. Joaquin Jackson Texas Ranger retired and author at a benefit located at the Pioneer Museum in downtown Fredericksburg, Texas on 16 March 2013. (Author's photo)

15-7 Colt .45 ACP Lightweight Defender fully engraved with 3 inch stainless steel slide, ivory grips with carved FTRA badge by Jim Aliamo, Nutmeg Sports LLC. Author's daily carry gun. (Author's collection)

15-8 Former Texas Rangers Association membership certificate. (Author's Collection)

CHAPTER 16

STORIES I FORGOT TO TELL

When I wrote the first edition in 2015 and the second edition in 2016, I figured I had about covered the ground I needed to tell: The story of the guns of the Texas Rangers. Like most authors, I am consistently finding new stories and interesting guns to cover. Therefore, I am writing this third edition in 2017.

Captains Charles Stevens and Frank Hamer

Captain Charles Stevens commanded Company G in Brownsville, Texas and later in Marathon on August 16, 1918. He commanded Company G from 1917 to 1920. During this time period, Frank Hamer found himself out of the Rangers. He petitioned his old friend Capt. Stevens for a job and was hired by Capt Stevens as a Ranger in his Company G. Frank Hamer promoted to Sergeant in Company G. A strong friendship developed between Capt Stevens and Frank Hamer that lasted many years only ending in 1929 when Capt Stevens, then a Federal Prohibition officer was assassinated by a bootlegger and died in Bexar County. Capt Hamer was conducting raids in the Borger oil fields and left to serve as a pallbearer at Capt Stevens's funeral.

A Smith & Wesson revolver is pictured in this chapter. It is documented to Captain Stevens and has been researched and believed to have been given to him by Capt Hamer during the 1920's, most likely appropriated during the earlier Borger oil fields campaign to stop illegal gambling and bootlegging activities.

Another interesting story involving Capt Frank Hamer concerns Reverend P.B. Hill. Pierre Bernard Hill, in the 1930's was appointed Chaplain of the Texas Rangers by Governor Dan Moody. He later was appointed Captain and Chaplin of Texas Rangers by Attorney General Bill Sterling. Reverend Hill was a six gun toting Ranger and best of friends with Capt Frank Hamer. Reverend Hill was the father of the famous WW II pilot and flying Tiger, Tex Hill. The story is told to me by a friend that he was invited to Tex Hill's house so he could sign his Flying Tiger book. While there Tex Hill asked if he wanted to see his dad's Colt Peacemaker. When he retrieved it from his safe, my friend noticed highly decorated grips with gold coins and what looked like a twisted gold link. Tex told him his dad was with Frank Hamer when he coughed up this watch chain link that had for many years been lodged in his lung. During a shootout in Sweet Water, Texas in October 1917, a bullet hit Frank's watch chain and drove it into his lung. For obvious reasons, it was never removed. Reverend Hill took the link and had it added to his pistol grip. Reverend Hill is credited for writing the Texas Ranger prayer that is read at many current Texas Ranger events.

"When you see the devil, tell him a Ranger said, hello"

The final story in this chapter concerns guns, a kidnapping, a rescue and the death of a truly great and dedicated Texas Ranger. On 21 January 2017 I was in attendance at a memorial and monument dedication to the late Stan Guffey. The monument marker sits on the grounds of the Horseshoe Bay police department. Texas Ranger Stan Guffey gave his life in 1987 while rescuing two year old Kara Leigh Whitehead in Horseshoe Bay, Llano County. Ranger Guffey as well as my good friend, Ranger Johnnie Aycock concealed themselves in the rear passenger compartment of a Lincoln sedan that was left at the kidnapper's demand. The rear seat was removed and both Rangers hid in the darkened and highly vulnerable location. When the kidnapper entered the car with the little girl, he noticed Stan who identified himself as a Texas Ranger. In the gunfight that ensued, the kidnapper fatally wounded Stan with a stolen .44 magnum revolver. Stan somehow returned fire but did not hit the kidnapper. When his Colt 1911A1 pistol was found on the ground outside the Lincoln, it had been fired 3 times. In all the confusion that lasted only a few seconds, the kidnapper who could see Stan Guffey never really saw Ranger Aycock. Ranger Aycock was concealed and was wearing a military field jacket. He immediately started returning fire. He wasn't going to let this criminal get away. Taking into consideration the safety of the little girl, he continuously fired his 9mm Browning high power pistol through the driver's door and through the driver's side windshield in the area of the state inspection sticker. Upon final examination Ranger Aycock had continuously fired approximately 9 rounds and a total of 4 hitting the suspect. This was stated in the official report of investigation. Johnnie was focused and intent on his duty firing these 9 shots continually until he subdued the kidnapper.

I was recently told by Ranger Aycock that when he approached the dying kidnapper who was lying beside the car, he bent over and said "When you see the devil, tell him a Ranger said, hello." As soon as possible Ranger Aycock grabbed the little girl. Although scared and obviously confused, she never said a word. He comforted her and said words to the effect, "It's okay. I'm a Ranger." He then carried the little girl to safety. It should be noted that Ranger Aycock told me that he had a number of weapons with him while he was concealed in the passenger compartment. These included a 1911 Commander in .38 super, a 1911 Commander in .45 ACP, a Colt Python revolver, a .38 Smith & Wesson Chief revolver and the Browning 9mm high power. He stated the Browning was the closest weapon when he needed it so that is the one that was utilized.

For this selfless devotion to duty, Rangers Stan Guffey and Johnnie Aycock were awarded the DPS Medal of Valor: Stan Guffey's being awarded posthumously. The marble monument that currently stands in Horseshoe Bay honors the valor and dedication of Stan

Guffey and was long overdue. Many times in our busy lives we tend to forget the sacrifices and devotion to duty that our Rangers have given to their beloved Texas and its citizens. Texas Ranger Johnnie Aycock went on later to earn his second DPS Medal of Valor for rescuing another kidnapped child. He is the only recipient to have earned two medals out of only five total given to fellow Rangers. He is the most decorated Ranger in modern time, a humble man and honorable servant of Texas.

Just a side note in closing this chapter, my good friend and retired Texas Ranger H. Joaquin Jackson who is mentioned in Chapter 15, passed away of natural causes in June 2016. He was 80 years old. Joaquin was one of the old style Rangers who was not always politically correct but always a lawman of the highest integrity. There will never be another Ranger quite like him. I lost a good friend and Texas lost a legend.

CHAPTER 16

ILLUSTRATIONS

16-1 Texas Ranger Captains Charles Stevens and Frank Hamer on a busy street in Houston, Texas circa 1920's. Captain Stevens left the Rangers and became a supervisor with the Federal Prohibition service. (Authors collection)

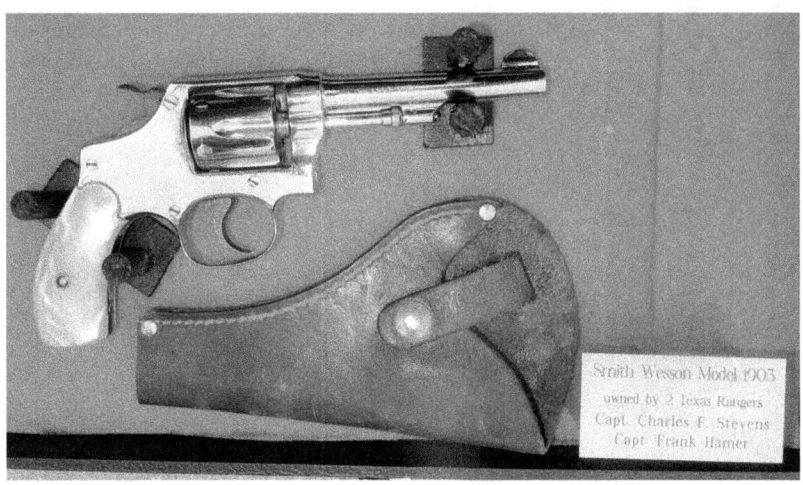

16-2 Smith & Wesson .32 cal hand ejector model of 1903 revolver. Nickel plated, back strap engraved "C Stevens," factory mother of pearl grips, gift of Capt Frank Hamer. (Authors collection)

16-3 Early photo of Texas Ranger Capt and Chaplin Pierre Bernard Hill. Reverend Hill shown mounted and wearing his Ranger six gun which he was known to use when needed circa 1930's. (Authors collection)

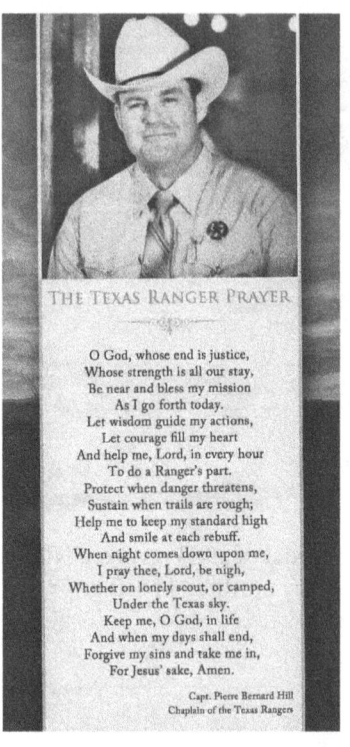

16-4 Copy of the Texas Rangers prayer as depicted on the memorial program for the Ranger Stan Guffey monument dedication at Horseshoe Bay, Texas. (Authors collection)

16-5 Browning Renaissance 9MM high power semi–automatic, top of the line for this model. A standard model was used in 1987 by Ranger Aycock. (Courtesy of John Aycock)

16-6 Retired Texas Ranger John Aycock and author holding his Winchester Model 1894 trapper carbine. Carbine was received from Ranger Kyle Dean and later personalized. (Authors collection)

16-7 M1, 30 caliber carbine with folding stock owned by Texas Ranger Sgt. John Aycock, Retired (Authors collection)

16-8 Close-up of personalized laser cut Ranger star of Texas Ranger John Aycock on the stock of trapper carbine. (Authors collection)

16-9 Colt Python, .357 magnum, 6 inch barrel with composite, Mexican eagle and snake grips. Documented to the late Texas Ranger H. Joaquin Jackson. (Authors collection)

16-10 The late Texas Ranger H. Joaquin Jackson and author at his home, Alpine, Texas 2015.

16-11 One of a kind custom engraved commemorative Bowie knife by Stories in Steel master engraver Sean McVicker to honor the life of the late Texas Ranger H. Joaquin Jackson

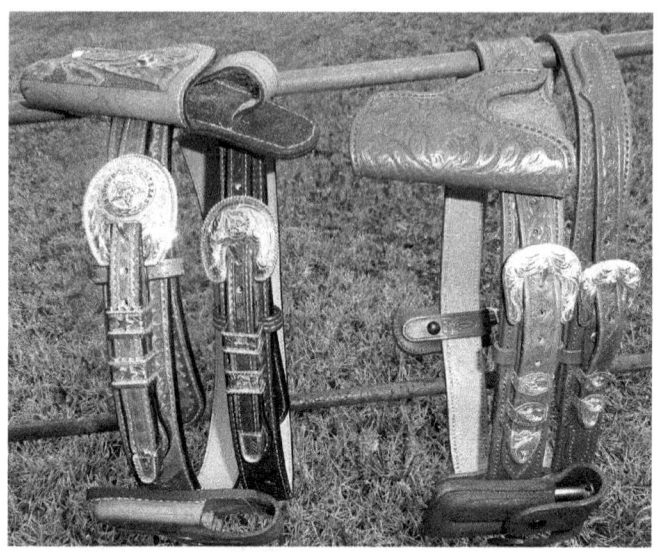

16-12 Two sets of classic Ranger leather pistol belts. *Left* – belt set with silver buckles and silver stars made by the inmate leather shop at Huntsville prison. Gift of Ranger John Aycock. *Right* – trouser belt and gun belt custom made to specifications used in the movie "Extreme Prejudice" which copied that of Ranger H. Joaquin Jackson. (Authors collection)

16-13 Two sets Texas Ranger leather, basket weave pattern with silver buckles, the other is an unusual oak leaf pattern with two holsters to fit the Beretta M92 pistol worn by retired Texas Ranger and former Ft. Bend County Sheriff, Milton Wright (Authors collection)

CHAPTER 17

MODERN TEXAS RANGER GUNS

For purposes of this narrative, I address modern guns as those made between 1960 and 2005. I did not address this area in previous chapters. As I am now writing my 3rd edition to the Texas Iron book and I have acquired knowledge on the subject, I decided to address it in this chapter.

In the 1940's and 1950's the standard handgun for law enforcement was the double action side ejecting .38 special revolver. Most popular in these was the Smith & Wesson and Colt produced versions. These two revolvers are pictured in Chapter 11. In the 1970's the revolver of choice for police departments to include the Texas DPS was the Smith & Wesson 357 magnum revolvers such as the Model 19, Model 27, Model 28-2 "Highway Patrol" model and the Model 586 to name a few. Remember that during this time the Texas Rangers were allowed to carry an appropriate weapon of their choice and most chose the Colt Model 1911A1 in Government and Commander styles. These were chambered to fire .45 ACP and .38 Colt super calibers.

As the era of automatics became more reliable and popular, po-lice departments began selecting models such as the Smith & Wesson Model 39 and Beretta M92 in .9MM to name a couple. Eventually the Texas Rangers replaced their Smith & Wesson Model 19's with the Sig Sauer Model P220 in .45 ACP. This was one of the "black guns" I men-tioned in an earlier chapter. Not much to look at, but highly reliable and accurate. Many Rangers still chose the Colt 1911's as their service carry weapons. DPS replaced the Sig Sauer P220 with the Sig Sauer model P226 chambered in the .357 Sig caliber. The .357 Sig cartridge is one of the finest calibers today. It is virtually a 9mm magnum being a .40

caliber casing bottle necked down to accept a 9mm projectile. Many Rangers like the performance and carried the P226 as a primary service weapon, while others stuck with their 1911s. Sometime around 2006 the Texas Department of Public Safety decided to replace the double action/single action P226s in .357 sig caliber with the double action only P226 in 9mm. I can only assume this was a decision based on logistics and cost as the .357 bullets can be pricey at times. In my opinion the 9mm version is a less desirable model. Again many Rangers chose to carry their Colt 1911s which was allowed as long as their DPS issued service weapon was readily available. This many times meant its storage in the trunk of their state issued vehicle. As times and technology increased, the Colt 1911s have in some instances been replaced for personal carry by newer equivalent models such as the Glock 17, 33 and equivalent pistols. Major Jeff Collins chose the Para Ordinance 1911, .45 ACP which utilized a 14 round magazine while working the border.

As for rifles of the time, the Winchester Model 1894 carbines in 30/30 caliber were in use way beyond expectation. An interesting story was told to me by retired Ranger Brantley Foster regarding the state provided Winchester Model 94s. During the final era of the Model 94, the Texas Ranger companies were said to paint a portion of the rifle stock to designate which company it was issued: one company red, one blue and so on. So I was told if I came across a model 94 with a red stock it might be a Texas Ranger gun. The Winchester semi-loaders and Remington semi-automatic Model 8 and Model 81 had a long and useful run also. In the early 1980s, the Texas DPS began purchasing the Sturm Ruger mini-14, semi-automatic rifles. These were the law enforcement models chambered in .223 caliber. They were purchased in blue and stainless steel versions, some with fixed wood stocks and some with factory folding stocks. The DPS purchased additional folding stocks and Ranger John Aycock remembers having his fixed wood stock replaced by a DPS folding model. Some Rangers liked the Mini 14s and some didn't. The Ruger Mini 14s did see a respectable service time period and saw use after the Colt AR15s came into service. The Ruger Mini 14s were first produced in the 1970s and commercial models are still marketed today. Again technology is constantly changing and new and more lethal models appear each year. It is for this reason that I will end the modern gun chapter here. For an old soldier like me, we can just get so modern before we have to halt in place.

CHAPTER 17

ILLUSTRATIONS

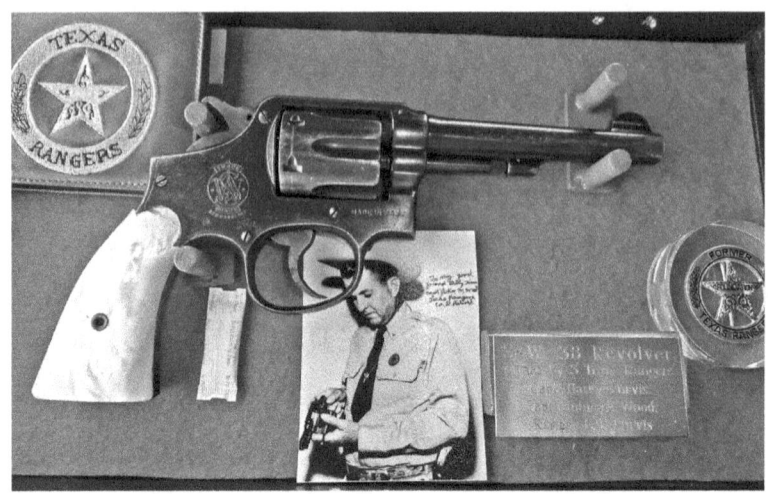

17-1 Smith & Wesson .38 military and police Model 10 revolver with mother of pearl grips. Documented to three Texas Rangers: Capt John M. Wood, Capt Hardy B. Purvis and Sgt L. H. Purvis. (Authors collection)

17-2 Pair of Smith & Wesson Model 19s with left and right holsters documented to the late Texas Ranger Captain G.W. Burks, B Company. Pistols have hammer spurs removed, actions accurized and double action only. One was DPS issue and one private purchase. (Authors collection)

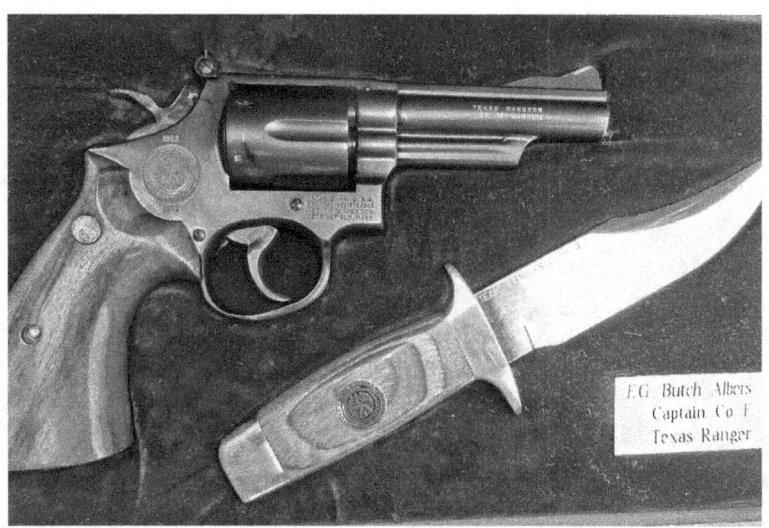

17-3 Smith & Wesson Model 19, Texas Ranger commemorative set. Documented to the late Captain Butch Albers who actually carried this revolver as his service weapon in 1973. (Authors collection)

17-4 Sig Sauer Model P220 in .45 ACP. Documented DPS issue service pistol for retired Texas Ranger Lieutenant Joe Hutson. He served as a Texas Ranger from 1996 to 2009. (Authors collection)

17-5 Sig Sauer Mode P226 in .357 sig caliber. Documented DPS issue service pistol for retired Texas Ranger Sergeant Ronnie Griffith, Company B. He served as a Texas Ranger for 28 years retiring in 2010. (Authors collection)

17-6 Special Texas Ranger Edition Beretta M92. Produced by permission of Texas DPS for serving Rangers. Less than 40 were purchased. The above pistol serial number 14 reflects Lieutenant Bob Favor's seniority in 1984. (Authors collection)

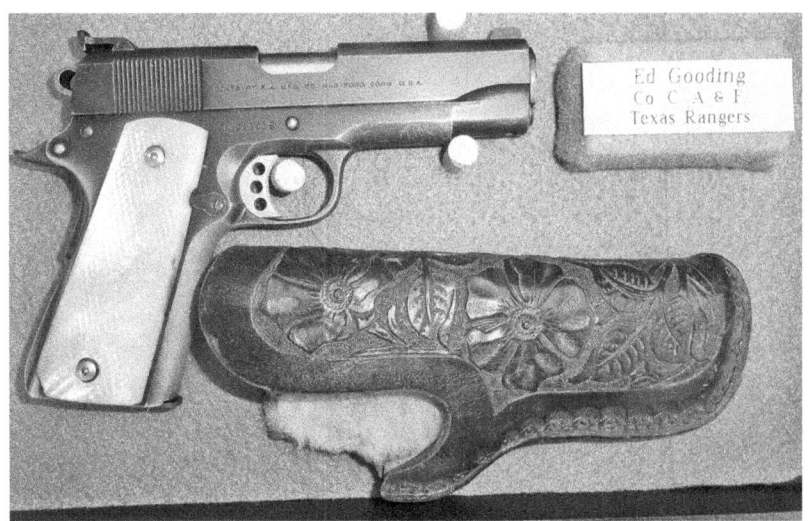

17-7 Colt Lightweight Commander .45 ACP with mother of pearl grips. Documented to the late Texas Ranger Ed Gooding who served 34 years in law enforcement, retiring in 1982. (Authors collection)

17-8 Colt Model 1911A1 Documented to retired Texas Ranger Sgt. Kyle L. Dean, Co F. Customized in dull stainless finish, accurized action with unusual S&W K frame adjustable sights. Kyle Dean served as a Ranger from 1992 to 2008. He is the son of retired Ranger Captain and U.S. Marshall Jack Dean. (Authors collection)

17-9 Colt Combat Commander, stainless steel, known as a concealed carry officer model (CCO) .45 ACP and is one of 500 made in 1991 with badge. Documented to retired Texas Ranger Sgt Steve Boyd who served as a Ranger from 1997 to 2011. During his time as a DPS trooper he was awarded the commissioners Medal of Valor. (Authors collection)

17-10 Pistol, M1911A1, Colt licensed Argentine police Model of 1927. Engraved and carried by retired Ranger Sgt Doyle Holdridge. Trigger guard removed as was the style of the famous Ranger Frank Hamer and Lone Wolf Gonzaules. (Authors collection)

17-11 Glock, Model 33, Gen 3 in .357 Sig, law enforcement model with gold Major badge. Documented to retired Texas Ranger Major Shawn Palmer who used it as a backup weapon. He served in the Rangers from 2001 to 2014. (Authors collection)

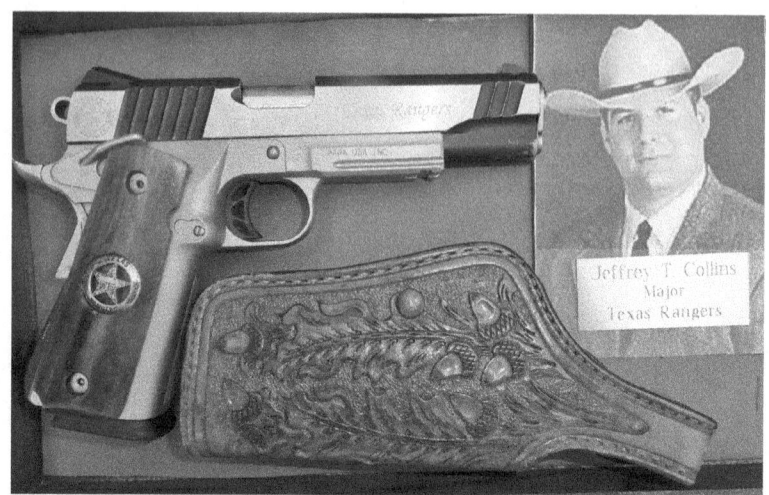

17-12 Para Ordnance, high capacity 1911, .45 ACP with 14 round magazine. Documented to currently serving Major Jeffrey T. Collins who carried it as a Lieutenant leading a Special Response Team from 2008 to 2012. (Authors collection)

17-13 Colt Lightweight Commander, .45 ACP pistol reworked by Houston, Texas gunsmith, Ed Vandenberg, silver & gold Mexican grips. Documented to currently serving Texas Ranger Lt. Chris Clark, Co E, Midland, Texas. (Authors collection)

17-14 Colt Lightweight Defender, stainless steel slide, .45 ACP. Documented to serving Texas Ranger Sgt Mike Smith, Co C, Pampa, Texas. (Authors collection)

17-15 Sturm Ruger, Mini-14, stainless Law Enforcement Model in .223 caliber, with factory folding stock. Documented to retired Texas Ranger Sgt Steve Foster. He was issued it as his DPS service rifle in June 1996. He served as a Ranger from 1996 to 2008. (Authors collection)

17-16 Winchester, Model 1892, trapper carbine with 16 inch barrel in 44/40 WCF caliber manufactured in 1911. Reworked and carried by Texas Ranger Sgt. Ronald C. Stewart while serving in Co. F. Displayed with vintage saddle scabbard, trapper size, maker marked Brownsville, Texas. (Authors collection)

17-17 Colt Combat Commander, .45 auto, stainless, Cogan custom with ivory grips inscribed "Texas Ranger Capt Jack Dean." Owned and carried by retired Texas Ranger and US Marshall Jack Dean. (Authors collection)

17-18 Colt Gold Cup National Match .45 auto with silver Texas Ranger grips, engraving by David Harris. Owned and carried by retired Texas Ranger Sgt. James R. (Jim) Huggins.

CHAPTER 18

BADGES AND HANDCUFFS

Badges

It is sometimes hard to accept, given the wide coverage of western Hollywood movies, but contrary to modern portrayals, 19th century Rangers did not wear badges. There was not a centralized standard badge for the Texas Rangers until 1935 with the creation of the Texas Department of Public Safety. In fact frontier Rangers in 1874 used a document titled "A warrant of authority" and was issued by the Texas adjutant general's office. Officers kept this paper document folded in their pockets as proof of authority. Initially Texas Ranger Privates were not allowed to make an arrest. This obviously later changed. As mentioned in 1935, with the creation of DPS a standardized Ranger badge was established. If a frontier Ranger did display a badge it was most likely a one of a kind locally manufactured variety of the star and wheel design. These were fashioned from a Mexican silver 8 Reales coin. I have two badges made from an 8 Reales coin with both coins dated in the 1890's. The current present day Cinco peso badge was fashioned after the 8 Reales badges. Some people think the Cinco peso badge used today is made from the same Reales coin. Although of the same size with both having similar silver content (8 Reales coin having over 90% pure silver). The term "pieces of eight" came from the early practice of subdividing this coin sometimes into eight pieces. The Cinco peso coin is however a more modern striking. The Mexican

5 peso, Cinco peso, used in todays badges was only produced in the years 1947 and 1948. The belief is that late G.W. Burks, Captain Co. B was interested in badges. He commissioned a version of the star and wheel badge in the fashion of the 8 Reales badges. He showed it to Capt. Bob Mitchell who also liked the design. They sent the badge to Austin to Homer Garrison, Jr., the director of the DPS. Col Garrison liked the design and after a period of time the Cinco peso badge was approved for wear in 1962. This replaced the unpopular blue and silver "bottle cap" badge. The bottle cap Ranger badge was approved in 1957. It was so unpopular, many veteran Rangers wore their one piece silver "saddle bag" or shield badge that was approved in 1935. It was oval shaped and contained the legend "Dept. of Public Safety, T-E-X-A-S" and a star in the center. Captains were issued gold badges and lower ranks silver. As mentioned, in 1957 DPS authorized a new badge design known by some as a "bottle cap" or "cracker jack" badge. It was an oval solid badge with a 5 pointed star surrounded with a royal blue background with silver or gold letters spelling Texas. The lettering in the outer ring is also in royal blue. It cannot be understated how unpopular this badge was with the Rangers. In 1962 when a Cinco peso star and wheel badge was authorized for wear there was almost unanimous acceptance by the Rangers. This was a popular decision and to present day this steeped Mexican silver badge is the symbol of the Texas Rangers. Each newly appointed Ranger is presented a Cinco peso badge upon his oath of enlistment by the director of the DPS. The five pointed star symbolizes the "Lone Star" of Texas. The olive branch on the right signifies peace and the oak leaves on the left, signifies strength. This badge is also known as the wagon wheel badge. Special Rangers were authorized a Cinco peso badge with the designation "Special Ranger." Personalized badges were later authorized with the Rangers name on the top in lieu of the Dept of Public Safety wording. The rest of the badge is standard. Virtually all Cinco peso badges display a concave shape although a later "flat badge" was known to have been worn and presented by some of the Ranger Captains.

Handcuffs

Included in the illustrations at the end of this chapter are a number of vintage handcuffs. The 19th century Hiatt-Darby 104 nickel single locking position cuffs had a key that more resembled a tool. When inserted it was merely turned until is released the cuff section. The cuffs are stamped with the number 14 which is believed to be the officer's divisional number. The other vintage set, an early adjustable style of handcuffs marked Mattatuck Mfg Co. Watertown, Conn are from circa 1920's and belonged to Texas Ranger Duke Hudson who joined the Texas Ranger in 1906 with Frank Hamer. It was one of the first practical key operated adjustable handcuffs. The Smith & Wesson and American Munitions Co. sets illustrated in this chapter represent the cuffs used extensively in the 1960's through the 1980's and are still used today.

What has become popular today however is the use of disposable nylon type restraints very similar to a nylon tie used to bundle wire or hold hardware items. One reason for the popularity of "one time use restraints" is first cost and secondly the transfer of a prisoner is less complicated without having to remove and secure arresting officers handcuffs. Many officers have conveyed stories to me of losing their handcuffs during process of prisoner hand off or transfer. Also illustrated in the chapter is a highly decorated set of engraved Colt handcuffs. Both have a floral design with one engraved "Texas Ranger" and the other "Department of Public Safety." This highly ornamental set of cuffs is believed to have been presented to the late F Co. Capt Butch Albers. This type of cuff, if worn at all, would most likely be for ceremony or events where BBQ guns would be on display.

As a closing story, there was recently a sale listing for a set of handcuff and leg iron restrains that were purportedly used in the 1920s by the Bexar sheriff's department to hold a well known Mexican bandit. It was interesting to note that the cuffs and leg irons remained on the bandit during his somewhat lengthy stay. It is hard to imagine that modern day jailers could get away with such a thing. Today the human rights advocates would object, however, in the days of old the "wild ones" would wear restraints for the duration of their incarceration if it was felt necessary to do so. We have come a long way from the days of iron cuffs and leg irons to the current era of the nylon ties.

Well again we find ourselves at the end of another journey. I hope the added information I have included in this Third Edition, Chapters 16, 17 and 18, will be a welcome addition to understanding the great heritage given to Texas by the Texas Rangers. This will be my final addition to the Texas Iron book. It has been my privilege to have the distinction of writing the first historical reference where the central subject throughout time is the guns carried by the Texas Rangers. In closing I will say God bless Texas, the Texas Rangers and all the Sons and Daughters who love and respect our great State.

CHAPTER 18

ILLUSTRATIONS

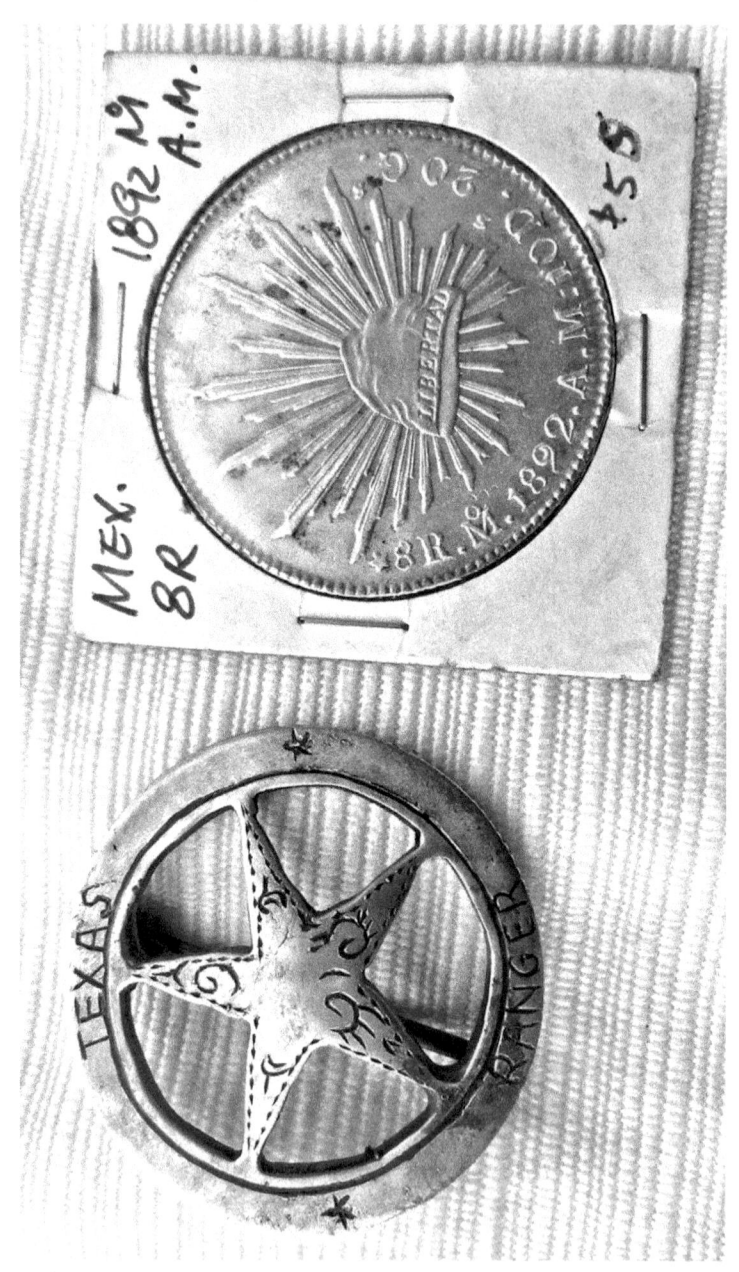

18-1   Early 1900 Texas Ranger Privates badge made from Mexican 8 Reales coin which is dated 1894. 90% pure silver – an example of a mint 8 Reales coin dated 1892 also illustrated. (Authors collection)

18-2 Early State Hwy Patrolman's badge circa 1935. This was the first State Highway Patrol badge authorized by the new DPS. It has a Dayton Company hallmark stamp on the rear side. (Authors collection)

18-3 Two early non standard Ranger badges. The "Hq" badge made from early 8 Reales coin. Dept of Public Safety badge made from cinco peso and was owned by the late Capt. Bob Mitchell (Authors collection)

18-4 Authorized Ranger badges since establishment of DPS in 1935. L – R Silver shield or ""saddle bag (1935-57), blue and silver "bottle cap" (1957-62), current Cinco peso badge (1962 to present) with 1947 Cinco peso coin. (Authors collection)

18-5 Grouping of current Texas Ranger Cinco peso badges. Top – Gold Captains badge owned by G.W. Burks, and personalized Majors badge of Shawn Palmer. Bottom – Silver / Private, Sergeant and Lieutenant badges. (Authors collection)

WILSON E. SPEIR
Director
LEO E. GOSSETT
Assistant Director

TEXAS DEPARTMENT OF PUBLIC SAFETY
TEXAS RANGERS
INTERSTATE 35 WEST, BOX 6167
WACO, TEXAS 76706

Commission
WILLIAM B. BLAKEMORE, II
Chairman
OTTIS E. LOCK
ROBERT R. SHELTON

COMPANY F

STATE OF TEXAS)(

COUNTY OF MCLENNAN)(

TO WHOM IT MAY CONCERN:

This Texas Ranger Captain's badge was presented by me to Mr. Hugh C. Cole of McAllen, Texas. Mr. Cole has my permission to display this badge with his other Ranger badges, guns and memorabilia.

Robert K. Mitchell, Captain
Texas Rangers, Company "F"
Waco, Texas

Signed and sworn to before me a Notary Public in and for the County of McLennan, State of Texas, this the 31st day of December 19 75.

Notary Public
McLennan County

18-6 Lucite encased documentation and gold Captains badge belonging to the late Texas Ranger Bob Mitchell who commanded F Co., Waco. Notarized document dated 1975. (Authors collection)

18-7 Former Texas Rangers commemorative badges left and middle are Former Texas Ranger Foundation, right is Charles Schreiner III badge. (Authors collection)

18-8 Badge and rubber mold used to cast it. Badge reads "Texas State Peace Officer" made at the Hughes unit Gatesville State Prison. (Courtesy of John Aycock)

18-9 Close-up of mold used to make Ranger Badge. Mold reads "Dept of Public Safety, Co. F, Texas Rangers" – made at the Hughes unit Gatesville State Prison. (Courtesy of John Aycock)

18-10 Commemorative 75th Anniversary Gold and Blue Texas Ranger badge offered for a limited time through permission of the DPS. Badge reads "75th anniversary, Department of Public Safety, Texas Rangers, Sergeant." On the left is a Ranger millennium badge. (Courtesy of John Aycock)

18-11 Two Texas prison system correctional officer badges, prison made and one is for the Texas Alcohol Beverage Commission agent. (Authors collection)

18-12 Vintage early handcuffs – Top – early nickel plated adjustable handcuff set manufactured by Mattauck Mfg Co Watertown, Conn ; circa 1920s. Used by late Texas Ranger Duke Hudson. Bottom – very early single locking position nickel plated cuffs marked Hiatt Darby circa 1880s – 1910. (Authors collection)

18-13 Two modern sets of hand cuffs – Top – Smith & Wesson stainless steel cuffs; Bottom black finish federal government purchase marked American Munitions Company. (Authors collection)

18-14 Engraved set of presentation Colt Mfg handcuffs. Colt authorized a sub-contractor to produce these in the 1970/1980s. This highly engraved set marked "Department of Public Safety and Texas Ranger." Believed to have been presented to the late Capt Butch Albers. (Authors collection)

18-15 Leg or ankle restraints used for short term prisoner transport, military set dated 1945. (Authors collection)

Bibliography

This work relies heavily on my personal knowledge after many years of studying the Texas Rangers and antique American firearms. Interviews and discussions make up an integral portion of this work. I am grateful to the individuals listed at the end of this section for their assistance and professional knowledge that enabled me to complete this book.

Books

Adler, Dennis, *Colt 175 Years, The History of Americas Premier Gun Maker*, Metro Books, New York, Copyright 2012.

Bady, Donald B., *Colt Automatic Pistols*, Pioneer Press, Copyright 2000

Boessenecker, John, *Texas Ranger-The Epic Life of Frank Hamer*, Thomas Dunne Books Copyright 2016

Cox, Mike, *Texas Ranger Tales*, Republic of Texas Press, Copyright 1997

Cox, Mike, *Time of the Texas Rangers*, Tom Doherty Associates, LLC, Copyright 2009

Day, James M., *Clint Peoples, Texas Ranger*, Texas Press, Waco, Copyright 1980.

Elliot, Glenn, *A Texas Ranger*, Texas Press, Waco, Texas, Copyright 1999

Flayderman, Norm, *Flayderman's Guide to Antique American Firearms and Their Values*, Krause Publications, 8th Edition, Copyright 2001.

Gillett, James B., *Six Years With The Texas Rangers*, University of Nebraska Press, Copyright 1921, 1925, 1976.

Glassard, Bruce A and Harold Weiss, Jr., *Tracking the Texas Rangers, The Nineteenth Century*, University of North Texas Press, Copyright 2012.

Glassard, Bruce A and Harold Weiss, Jr., *Tracking the Texas Rangers, The Twentieth Century*, University of North Texas Press, Copyright 2013.

Gooding, Ed, *Soldier Texas Ranger*, Ranger Publishing, Copyright 2001.

Harris, Charles H. III, Harris, Frances E., Sadler, Louis R., *Texas Ranger Biographies 1910 – 1921*, University of New Mexico Press, Copyright 2009.

Jackson, H. Joaquin, *One Ranger – A Memoir*, University of Texas Press, Austin, Copyright 2005.

Jackson, H. Joaquin, *One Ranger Returns*, University of Texas Press, Austin, Copyright 2008.

Martinez, Ramiro (Ray), *They Call Me Ranger Ray*, Rio Bravo Publishing, Copyright 2010.

Mills, Susie, *Legend in Bronze Biography of Jay Banks*, Ussery Printing Company, Copyright 1982.

Myatt, Frederick (Major), *Illustrated Encyclopedia of Pistols and Revolvers*, Crescent Books, New York, Copyright 1980.

O'Meara, Robert H. (Doc), *Colts Single Action Revolver*, Krause Publications, Copyright 1999

Parsons, Chuck, *John B. Armstrong*, Texas A&M University Press, Copyright 2007.

Ringler, Lewis C. and Judyth W., *In The Line of Duty*, University of North Texas Press, Copyright 1984.

Robinson, Charles M. III, *The Men Who Wear the Star*, Modern Library, Copyright 2000.

Spinks, S. E., Law on the *Last Frontier/Texas Ranger Arthur Hill*, Texas Tech University Press, Copyright 2007.

Tanner, Hans (Editor), *Guns of the World*, Bonanza Books, Pettersen Publishing Co., Copyright 1972, 1977

Utley, Robert M., *Lone Star Justice*, Berkley Publishing Group, Copyright 2002.

Utley, Robert M., *Lone Star Law Men—The Second Century*, Berkley Books, New York, Copyright 2007.

Webb, Walter Prescott, *The Texas Rangers*, University of Texas Press, Austin, Copyright 1935/1965/1991.

Personal Interviews

Albers, E.G. Jr., Captain, Company F, Texas Rangers (ret) interview 1983

Aycock, Johnnie, Sgt. Texas Rangers (ret), Company F, verbal interviews 2015 – 2017

Block, H.R. (Lefty), Sr. Capt, Texas Rangers (ret) verbal interview 2016.

Boessenecker, John, Author and authority on law enforcement, email interview 2016.

Casteel, Bruce, Sr. Capt. Texas Rangers (ret) verbal interview 2015.

Clark, Chris, Lt. Texas Rangers, Companies A, B, F & Hq, verbal interviews 2016-2017.

Cox, Mike, Author, Historian of Texas Ranger Foundation, verbal interview 2016.

Davis, Joe, Sgt. Texas Rangers (ret), Company F, verbal interviews 2014-2017.

Favor, Bob, Lt. Texas Rangers (ret), Company D, phone interview 2017.

Foster, Brantley, Sgt. Texas Rangers (ret), Company B, verbal interview 2015.

Gooding, Ed, Sgt Texas Rangers (ret), Interview 1983.

Hamer, Harrison, Hamer family historian, San Saba, Texas, verbal interviews 2016-2017.

Jackson, H. Joaquin, Author, actor, Sgt. Texas Rangers (ret), Company E. verbal interviews 2014 – 2016.

Johnson, Byron, Texas Ranger Hall of Fame, Waco, Curator, interviews, 2015 – 2016.

Martinez, Ray, Sgt. Texas Rangers (ret), Company D, interviews 2015 – 2017.

Miller, Morgan, Sgt. Texas Rangers, (ret) Company D, phone interview 2016.

Sessums, Grady, Capt. Texas Rangers (ret), verbal interviews 2014-2016.

Stewart, Ronald C., Sgt. Texas Rangers (ret) Companies F, E and Hq, verbal interview 2017.

Villalobos, Gerald, Sgt. Texas Rangers (ret), Company E, verbal interviews 2016.

Weathers, Carl, Capt. Texas Rangers (ret), Company A, C, verbal interviews 2015 – 2017.

INDEX

A

Alamo, 19
Albers, Butch, 169, 193
Armstrong, Charlie, 99
Armstrong, John B., 64, 70, 71, 76
Arrington, William, 25
Aston, Henry, 36
Austin, Stephen F., 17
Aycock, Johnnie, 145, 148, 149, 154

B

Banks, Capt. Jay, 118, 128
Barrow, Clyde, 107, 117
Bass, Sam, 71
Bean, Judge Roy, 79
Bowie, Jim, 24
Burks, G. W. Captain, 170, 180, 187
Burton, Isaac, 25

C

Callahan, James H., 43, 44
Carmichael, Horace, 119, 122
Cinco Peso Badge, 186, 187
Coacoochee, Wild Cat, 43
Colt, Patterson Fire Arms, 26, 30, 31
Colt, Samuel, 27
Comanche, Indians, 17, 25, 91, 92
Cortez, Gregorio, 97

D

Davis, Joe B., 113, 119
Davis, "Rangers 1870," 62
DeLaPena, Enrique, 19
Dillinger, John, 100
Dove Creek, 54

E

El Paso, Texas, 79, 90
Estelle, Jim, 108

F

Ferguson, Governor Ma, 110
Fisher, John King, 71
Flintlock Fire Arms, 19
Ford, John Salmon, 51
Foster, Brantley, 120, 144, 166

G

Garrison, Homer, 119, 128, 130
Gillett, James B., 72
Gonzaullas, "Lone Wolf," 109, 127
Gray, Mabry B, 20
Guffey Stan, 154

H

Hamer, Frank, 108, 109
Hardin, John Wesley, 69, 70, 71
Hayes, John C., 26, 33, 35, 97
Hickman, Tom, 109, 110, 127
Hill, Pierre Bernard, 154
Houston, Sam, 26
Hudson, R. M. (Duke), 98, 103
Hudson, Duke, 98, 192
Hughes, Capt. John, 98

I

Ivory Grips, 120

J

Jackson, Joaquin, 92, 100, 118, 146, 150, 151
Jackson, H. Joaquin, 92, 100, 118, 156, 163
Jay, Lieutenant, Co. A, 80
Johnson, Ira, 36
Jones, Major John B., 63, 79

K

Karnes, Henry W., 26
Kiowa Warriors, 20, 25

L
LaMat, Dr. Jean Alexander, 63
Longley, Bill, 71
Lucas, Weldon, 114, 143

M
Mason County, 63
McNelly, Leander H., 63, 91, 97
Merwin Herbert Arms, 72
Mueschke, Herman, 145

N
Nance, Jim, 133
Nueces Strip, 28, 30, 33, 82

O
Oakley, Annie, 81
Obregon, President Alvaro, 99

P
Parker, Bonnie, 107, 117
Parker Shotguns, 72, 77
Peoples, Capt. Clint, 128, 132
Piedras Negras, 43

R
Rancheros, 20
Rangers Corps, 17
Rangers, Former Texas Assn., 152
Rangers, Texas, 25, 44, 62
Remington Arms, 62
Ross, Saul, 52

S
Santa Anna, General, 27, 35
Schreiner, Charlie III, 110, 139
　Y.O. Ranch, 128
Smith, Deaf, 26
Stevens, Charles F., 153
Starr Arms, 57
Sterling, W.W. Bill, 127

T
Taylor, Zachary, 34
Terry's Texas Rangers, 89, 52
Thompson, John T., 108
Tumlinson, John T., 25

U
United States, Bureau of Ordnance, 51
United States, Texas annexed, 27

V
Vasquez, Rafael, 33
Villalobos, Gerald, 123, 124
Vivian, Leon T., 100

W
Walker Creek Battle, 26, 35
Walker, Samuel, 27, 33, 34
Waters, Asa, 19
White, Rollin, 69
Whitney, Eli, 42, 67
Winchester Fire Arms, 80, 81, 100, 120

www.ingramcontent.com/pod-product-compliance
Lightning Source LLC
Chambersburg PA
CBHW061603110426
42742CB00039B/2750